SONGS OF THE WILD WEST

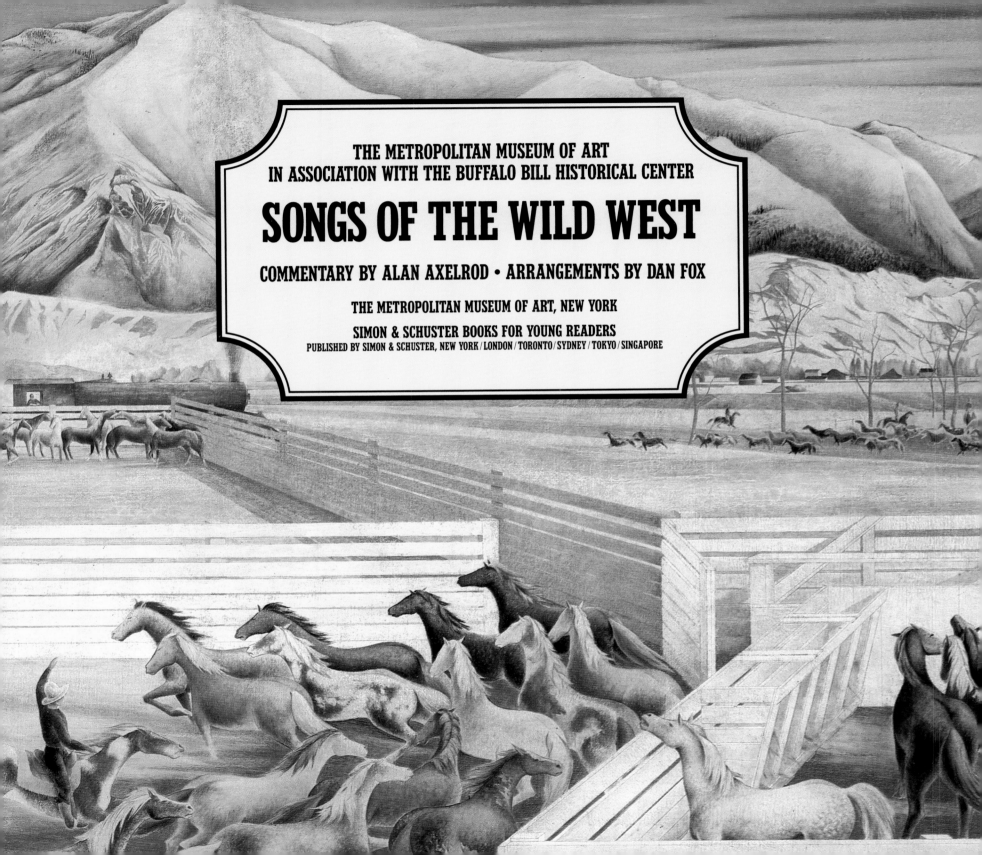

SONGS OF THE WILD WEST

THE METROPOLITAN MUSEUM OF ART
IN ASSOCIATION WITH THE BUFFALO BILL HISTORICAL CENTER

COMMENTARY BY ALAN AXELROD · ARRANGEMENTS BY DAN FOX

THE METROPOLITAN MUSEUM OF ART, NEW YORK

SIMON & SCHUSTER BOOKS FOR YOUNG READERS
PUBLISHED BY SIMON & SCHUSTER, NEW YORK / LONDON / TORONTO / SYDNEY / TOKYO / SINGAPORE

We gratefully acknowledge Peter H. Hassrick, Director of the Buffalo Bill Historical Center, Cody, Wyoming, and his staff for their cooperation and assistance in producing this book. Particular thanks are due Elizabeth Holmes, Assistant Registrar, Lillian Turner, Public Programs Coordinator, and Sarah E. Boehme, John S. Bugas Curator of the Whitney Gallery of Western Art.

Illustrations from the The Metropolitan Museum of Art are indicated by the abbreviation MMA; illustrations from the Buffalo Bill Historical Center are marked BBHC.

Front cover, left to right: *Rounding Up, Bucking,* and *The Wild Spectacular Race for Dinner.* Details of paintings by N.C. Wyeth, American, 1882–1945; oil on canvas, 1904–05; BBHC.

Back cover: *Cowboy Singing*; Thomas Eakins, American, 1844–1916; watercolor on paper; MMA.

Endpapers: *Head of a Bull*; Emanuel Wyttenbach, American, 1857–1894; lithograph; MMA.

Page 1: *So Goes the Dance*; Frederic Remington, American, 1861–1909; illustration from *Cosmopolitan*, April 1892, from *Frederic Remington, 1861–1909: Artist Historian of the Old West*, scrapbooks compiled by Helen L. Card; MMA.

Title page: *Last of the Wild Horses* (detail); Frank Albert Mechau, Jr., American, 1903–1946; oil on canvas, 1937; MMA.

Page 5: *Bronco Busters Saddling*; Frederic Remington, American, 1861–1909; illustration from *Century*, February 1888, from *Frederic Remington, 1861–1909: Artist Historian of the Old West*, scrapbooks compiled by Helen L. Card; MMA.

Published by The Metropolitan Museum of Art, New York, and
SIMON & SCHUSTER BOOKS FOR YOUNG READERS
Simon & Schuster Building, Rockefeller Center
1230 Avenue of the Americas
New York, New York 10020
SIMON & SCHUSTER BOOKS FOR YOUNG READERS is a trademark of Simon & Schuster.

Library of Congress Cataloging-in-Publication Data
Songs of the Wild West / commentary by Alan Axelrod ; arrangements by Dan Fox.
The Metropolitan Museum of Art in association with the Buffalo Bill Historical Center.
    Includes index.
    1. Cowboys—West (U.S.)—Songs and music. 2. Folk music—West (U.S.) 3. Folk songs, English—West
(U.S.) I. Axelrod, Alan, 1952–   . II. Fox, Dan. III. Metropolitan Museum of Art (New York, N.Y.)
IV. Buffalo Bill Historical Center
M1629.6.W5SX   1991   91-751467
ISBN 0-671-74775-4 (Simon & Schuster)
ISBN 0-87099-611-8 (MMA)

Produced by the Department of Special Publications,
The Metropolitan Museum of Art
Designed by Miriam Berman
Photography by The Metropolitan Museum of Art Photograph Studio,
Bob Weiglein and Devendra Shirkhande of the Buffalo Bill
Historical Center staff, and Schecter Lee (p. 9).
Printed in Singapore.
10 9 8 7 6 5 4 3 2 1

CONTENTS

A NOTE ON THE MUSIC AND GUITAR CHORDS

All the songs are suitable for beginning to intermediate musicians, and each is accompanied by guitar chords. A fingering chart for all the chords used in the book appears on page 128.

When the piano arrangement is in a key that is awkward for the guitar, capo instructions and alternate chords are given. After the capo is in place, the song should be played using the chords that appear in parentheses.

Guitar
American, made by C. F. Martin, ca. 1838
Various woods, with abalone and
ivory decoration
MMA

Trappers Saluting the Rocky Mountains
A. J. Miller, American, 1810–1874
Oil on canvas, ca. 1864
BBHC

INTRODUCTION

This book celebrates, in song and in art, the Old West—its cowboys and cowgirls, outlaws and prospectors, gunfighters and markswomen, railroad workers and cavalrymen, sodbusters and broncobusters. The forty-five songs included tell of the trials and the victories these folks experienced as they moved across the country settling the American frontier. The range and order of the songs chronicle the history of western expansion—from the rousing opening, a pioneer favorite, "Ho! Westward Ho!" to the poignant final ballad, "Old Texas," which laments the end of the range-cattle industry.

Few of those who first sang these songs were professional composers. They were pioneers and settlers, who brought folk tunes with them from back East. They were laborers, who invented songs to make the work go easier. They were cowboys, who sang to keep themselves company while riding the line, to calm restless cattle and bed them down for the night, or to break the boredom of the dreary bunkhouse. They were men and women who needed nothing more than a lively tune to dance to. They were storytellers singing a tale of Jesse James, the Wabash Cannonball, Billy the Kid, or that mean and

7

Tzit-idoatl
Apache fiddle
American, late 19th century
Agave stalk and horsehair
MMA

The Great West
Published by Currier & Ives
Color lithograph, 1870
MMA

ornery strawberry roan pony. They were white—many of them southerners who moved west after the devastation of the Civil War. They were black—almost one of every seven cowboys was an African American. They were Mexican. Each group contributed its own musical tradition, including Native Americans. Music was a central feature of daily life for the North American Indians, but the songs lose much of their meaning when removed from the religious or ceremonial occasions that produced them, and the melodies and rhythmic patterns are virtually impossible to reproduce in a simple form. The rich and complex musical heritage of the Native Americans is represented here in one song—a haunting Navajo lullaby called "The Rainbow Cradle."

Unlike the West's musicians, its painters and sculptors were often highly trained professionals. Many of them learned their craft in Europe, made their homes back in the urban East, and were simply visitors to the frontier. Some of the best-known western artists—W.H.D. Koerner, Frederic Remington, and Charles Schreyvogel, for example—were active after the wildest days of the Wild West had passed. They were really depicting the West as it had been twenty or forty years earlier.

Of course, there are exceptions to this. The most beloved of all western artists, Charles M. Russell, was a real cowboy, whose drawings and paintings were popular first and foremost with westerners like himself. Even though he started painting mostly to please his cowboy friends, his work quickly became famous in every region of the United States and abroad.

Also represented are artists like Thomas Eakins and Marsden Hartley, who are not usually associated with the West but were nonetheless inspired by its mystique or its landscape. There are also works by little-known, even anonymous, men and women whose illustrations decorated posters, cigar boxes, and other everyday items. Accompanying these are objects actually used by pioneers and cowboys, among them saddles, spurs, cooking utensils, and musical instruments.

In 1890, the U.S. Census Bureau reported that since so many people had come to the West, you could no longer look at a map, draw a line across the country, and say: This side is settled and this side is wilderness. Explored, surveyed, claimed, sold, bought, given away, fenced, the frontier was, the Census Bureau said, closed.

This came as quite a shock to a lot of folks back in 1890. For most Americans—for most of the world—the Old West was the land of great adventure, of untold hazards but unlimited possibilities, a romantic land in which a man or a woman could be free. The West called out of the American character all that was best in it—courage, optimism, energy, self-reliance, inventiveness, and sheer exuberance—and all that was worst— bigotry, greed, a carelessness that too often extended to people as well as the land itself. But, good or bad, the Old West epitomized America. Good or bad, it was so full of life that it became bigger than life. How could it now, suddenly, be "closed"?

The songs, paintings, sculptures, prints, and other objects in this book prove that the Old West remains wide open to us today. The songs and the art endure, and as long as we go on craving adventure, hungering after wildness, revering courage, and cherishing hope for a better future, we'll go on singing songs and admiring images of an Old West that, in fact, has never aged.

ALAN AXELROD

The Rocky Mountains, Lander's Peak
Albert Bierstadt, American, 1830–1902
Oil on canvas, 1863
MMA

HO! WESTWARD HO!

Merced River, Yosemite Valley
Albert Bierstadt, American,
1830–1902
Oil on canvas, 1866 MMA

"Ho! Westward Ho!" is an anthem of the pioneer spirit, and the magnificent landscapes of Albert Bierstadt are its icons. Although it was based on sketches the artist made on site, *Merced River, Yosemite Valley* was painted in his castlelike studio overlooking the Hudson River in Irvington, New York. It is a work of the imag-ination, imbued with religious feeling, an invitation to a paradise on earth, God's country. It is no ac-cident that the height of Bierstadt's enormous popularity coincided with the post–Civil War years of westward expansion, the period that saw the Homestead Act and the completion of the transcon-tinental railroad.

Brightly, like a polka

1. "The star of em-pire," po-ets say,
2. Our Pil - grim Fa - thers sang the song,

Ho! West-ward Ho!

1. "For -
2. Here

ev - er takes its on - ward way!"
right should tri - umph o - ver wrong!

Ho! West-ward Ho!

That
Still

*Guitar: Capo 3rd fret

(*Please turn the page.*)

11

The first line of the song alludes to Bishop Berkeley's early eighteenth-century verses "On the Prospect of Planting Arts and Learning in America." Berkeley wrote, "Westward the course of empire takes its way," picturing the westering progress of mankind as the final glorious and inevitable act in the great drama of human development. The opening line of Berkeley's poem was quoted—and, as here, misquoted—for the next two hundred years.

Actually, folks went west for many reasons: to get rich, to escape creditors, to evade the law, to own land, to gain a sense of freedom denied them in the crowded East. But whatever the particular reason, there was, as in Berkeley's poem, an abiding sense that Americans were fulfilling their destiny, marching toward a Promised Land for which they were the Chosen People.

Cody, the Boy Guide—Danger Ahead!
Illustration from a pamphlet for Buffalo Bill's Wild West Show, 1885
MMA

HO! WESTWARD HO! *(Continued)*

Additional verses:

3.
'Tis ever thus, the people cry,
  Ho! Westward Ho!
And from the eastern cities fly,
  Ho! Westward Ho!
To live on God's most glorious land,
  Ho! Westward Ho!
Where hearts and thoughts are ever grand,
  Ho! Westward Ho!
(Chorus)

4.
The western fields give thousands wealth,
  Ho! Westward Ho!
And yield to all a glowing health,
  Ho! Westward Ho!
For all inclined to honest toil,
  Ho! Westward Ho!
Secure their fortunes from the soil,
  Ho! Westward Ho!
(Chorus)

5.
We love the glorious western land,
  Ho! Westward Ho!
For here the people's hearts expand,
  Ho! Westward Ho!
And on the prairies broad and grand,
  Ho! Westward Ho!
We all can see Jehovah's hand,
  Ho! Westward Ho!
(Chorus and Final Chorus)

Final Chorus

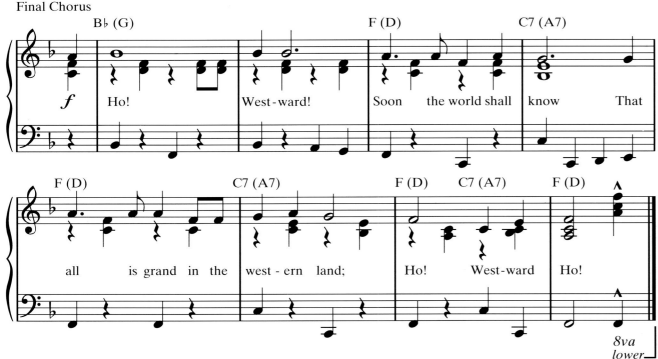

New Frontiers
The Society of Medalists 45th Issue
James Earle Fraser, American, 1876–1953
Bronze, 1952
MMA

A Home in the Wilderness
Published by Currier & Ives, New York
Hand-colored lithograph, 1870
MMA

13

ACROSS THE WIDE MISSOURI

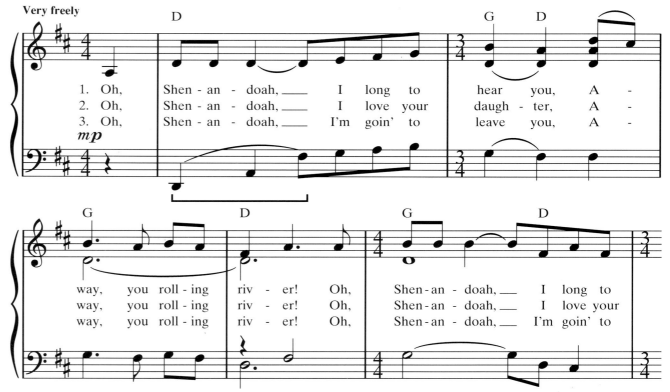

The westward urge of pioneer and settler was driven by mighty motives: a need for land, a search for wide-open spaces, an opportunity for wealth, the hope of greater liberty. But going to the West also meant leaving the East, forsaking the long familiar and the well loved for the new, the untried, and the hazardous. This extraordinarily beautiful song expresses the wayfarer's emotions in movingly simple terms.

Very freely

1. Oh, Shen - an - doah, ___ I long to hear you, A -
2. Oh, Shen - an - doah, ___ I love your daugh - ter, A -
3. Oh, Shen - an - doah, ___ I'm goin' to leave you, A -

way, you roll - ing riv - er! Oh, Shen-an-doah, ___ I long to
way, you roll - ing riv - er! Oh, Shen-an-doah, ___ I love your
way, you roll - ing riv - er! Oh, Shen-an-doah, ___ I'm goin' to

14

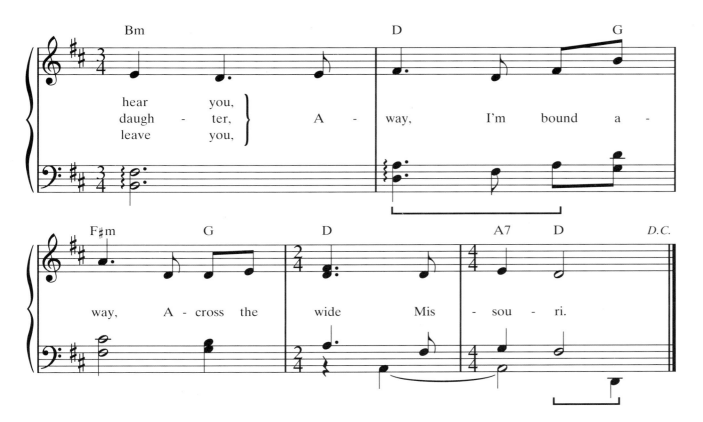

hear you,
daugh - ter, } A - way, I'm bound a -
leave you,

way, A - cross the wide Mis - sou - ri.

He exchanges one river, the Shenandoah, for another, the Missouri. Rolling through a fold of Virginia's Blue Ridge, the Shenandoah marks a portion of the continent's earliest western frontier. Rising in the Rocky Mountains of Montana, coursing through the Dakotas, forming the Nebraska-Iowa border, and winding down into Missouri to join the Mississippi River at St. Louis—embarkation point for the nation's new frontier—the Missouri River marked the entrance to the Far West.

Although *The Pioneer*, by the great eastern American painter Winslow Homer, is set not in Virginia's Shenandoah Valley but in the Adirondack Mountains of upstate New York, it does suggest the similarly gentle, well-forested landscape the westward-bound settler was leaving to risk his fortune—and his life—in the titanic country of the Missouri and beyond: a land vaster and wilder, but also less hospitable and more threatening.

William Jacob Hays, a New York artist best known for his quiet paintings of animals, fruit, and flowers, made one trip to the West, in 1860. Among many other paintings, that journey produced the magnificent view of the "wide Missouri" reproduced on the opposite page, which conveys something of the frontier's boundless promise and endless challenge.

A Herd of Bison Crossing the Missouri River
William Jacob Hays, Sr., American, 1830–1875
Oil on canvas, 1863
BBHC

The Pioneer
Winslow Homer, American, 1836–1910
Watercolor on paper, 1900
MMA

THE RAINBOW CRADLE

The Navajo Indians, who migrated into the Southwest from the plains sometime during the sixteenth century, were known and feared as a warlike people who habitually raided other Indians and Spanish colonists. In the nineteenth century, they also fought with American settlers and soldiers. Although it is customary to speak of a Navajo tribe, for most of their history the Navajo were loosely organized into small clans of kinsmen who lived close to one another so that they could easily cooperate in daily tasks.

Cradle
Cheyenne, ca. 1880
Deer hide, seed beads, trade cloth, ribbon, coins, brass bells, and wood   BBHC

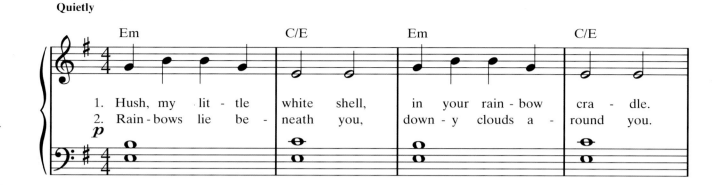

Quietly

1. Hush, my lit - tle white shell, in your rain - bow cra - dle.
2. Rain - bows lie be - neath you, down - y clouds a - round you.

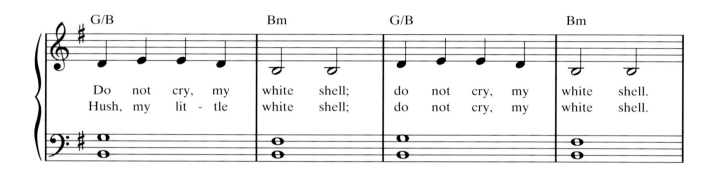

Do not cry, my white shell; do not cry, my white shell.
Hush, my lit - tle white shell; do not cry, my white shell.

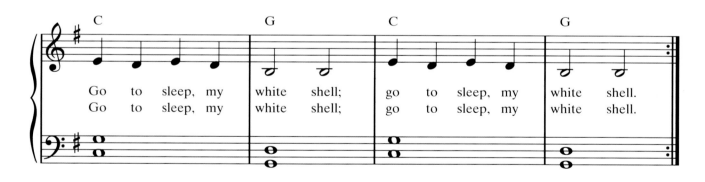

Go to sleep, my white shell; go to sleep, my white shell.
Go to sleep, my white shell; go to sleep, my white shell.

Last time

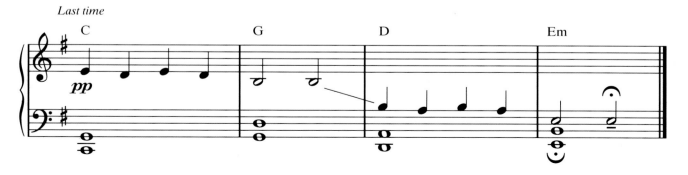

Aggressive and independent
though they were, the Navajo
developed close-knit, warm, and
caring families, as this gentle
lullaby suggests.

While Europeans and Americans
found it difficult to negotiate
treaties with the Navajo because
of their lack of central government,
the Navajo fared better than most
other Indian groups in confronta-
tion with white settlers and white
officials, securing a large and
prosperous reservation, today
totaling more than fifteen million
acres. They are also the most pop-
ulous single tribe, numbering
more than 100,000.

Navajo blanket
Arizona, ca. 1860
Wool
MMA

Navajo Family
F. Luis Mora, American, 1874–1940
Pencil on paper, 1905
MMA

OLD DAN TUCKER

"**O**ld Dan Tucker" was written by Dan Emmett, a backwoodsman of Irish descent who, in 1842, started something that became known as a minstrel show. Throughout the rest of the nineteenth century and well into the twentieth, these shows — staged by white men who, blacking their faces with burnt cork, sang, danced, and swapped jokes — were enormously popular.

The Mountain Man
Frederic Remington, American, 1861–1909
Bronze; 1903, this cast, 1907
MMA

Square dance tempo

mf

1. I
2. Now

G ... **C** ... **G** ... **D7**

went down-town ___ the oth-er night, I heard ___ a noise ___ and I saw ___ a fight. The
Old Dan Tuck-er is come to town, ___ Rid-in' a bil - ly goat and lead-in' a hound. The

G ... **C** ... **G** ... **C G**

watch-man, he was run-nin' ___ round, Cry-in': "Old Dan Tuck-er's ___ come ___ to town!"
hound dog bark, the bil-ly goat jump, Land-ed Old Dan Tuck-er on top of the stump.

Chorus
G ... **C** ... **D7** ... **G C G**

Get out the way, Old Dan Tuck-er, You're too late to get your sup-per.
f

18

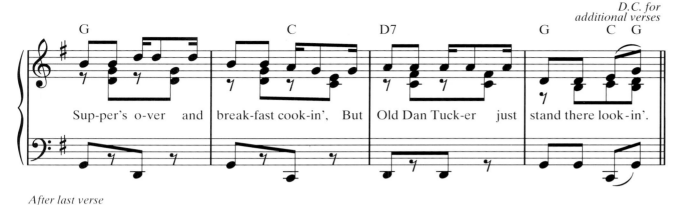

D.C. for additional verses

G   C   D7   G   C   G

Sup-per's o-ver and break-fast cook-in', But Old Dan Tuck-er just stand there look-in'.

After last verse

G   N.C.

ff   *sfz*

Additional verses:

3. Old Dan Tucker went down to the mill
   To get some meal to put in the swill.
   The miller swore by the point of his knife
   That he never seen such a man in his life.
   (Chorus)

4. Old Dan Tucker, he got drunk,
   Fell in the fire and kicked up a chunk.
   A red-hot coal rolled in his shoe,
   And oh my gosh how the ashes flew!
   (Chorus)

5. Old Dan Tucker was a fine old man,
   Washed his face in a frying pan,
   He combed his hair with a wagon wheel,
   Died with a toothache in his heel.
   (Chorus)

6. Now Old Dan Tucker is come to town
   Swingin' the ladies round and round.
   First to the right and then to the left,
   Then to the girl that he loves best.
   (Chorus)

7. Old Dan and me, we did fall out,
   And what do you think it was about?
   He stepped on my corn, I kicked his shin,
   And that's the way it all begin.
   (Chorus)

Skillet
American, 18th or 19th century; iron MMA

A Trapper; Frederic Remington, American, 1861–1909
Color lithograph from *A Bunch of Buckskins: Eight Drawings in Pastel by Frederic Remington,* published by R. H. Russell, New York, 1901 MMA

Emmett appropriated an African-American plantation tune for his song, and Old Dan was portrayed in the minstrel shows as a black vagabond who was scorned by everyone yet kept bouncing back with a kind of nonsensical magic. This kind of cockeyed exaggeration was especially cherished by frontier people and westerners, and Old Dan's popularity went far beyond the minstrel shows and the song. Tales appeared about him as if he were a real person, and best-selling joke books were named after him.

Why was this character so popular? Most likely, people saw in Old Dan Tucker a comic version of what they saw and admired in real-life heroes like Daniel Boone and Davy Crockett. Feisty, hard-drinking, vulgar, and bigger than life, Dan refused to conform to the civilized ways of the "town." After his eccentric fashion, Old Dan Tucker represented the freedom of the West itself.

An old prospector reminisces over the California gold rush of 1849 and the rough-and-ready comrades who forsook everything —home, family, employment—in hopes of striking it rich. The fact is that few ventures were as miserable as the business of prospecting, and, despite this song, few prospectors, miserable as they might be, sought comradeship: A friend might jump your claim just as fast as an enemy. Stories of instant riches, of nuggets lying on the ground waiting to be picked up, or of gold dust wanting only to be washed free of sand and dirt, lured hundreds of thousands to California.

It is true that, in the earliest days of the gold rush, all one had to do was shovel "pay dirt" onto a blanket and toss it into the air to winnow the dirt from the heavier gold dust. But such surface-deposited ore, called placer gold, was very quickly exhausted. Thousands of men scooped up dirt in a pan, immersed it in the water of a stream, lifted it out, and swirled it endlessly, tediously, hoping to detect a few grains of gold dust settled at the bottom of the pan. It was back-breaking work that yielded at most a few dollars a day, usually less.

Panning Gold, Wyoming
William R. Leigh, American, 1866–1955
Oil on canvas, 1949
BBHC

THE DAYS OF '49

*Guitar: Capo 3rd fret

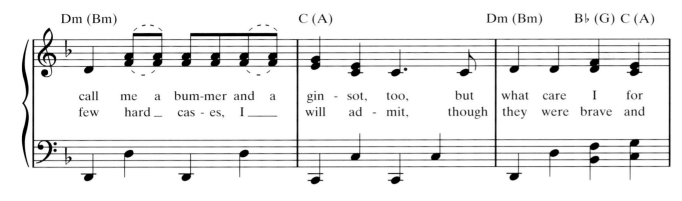

call me a bum-mer and a | gin - sot, too, but | what care I for
few hard ___ cas - es, I ___ | will ad - mit, but though | they were brave and

praise? I | wan - der a - round from | town ___ to town just
true. What | -ev - er the pinch they | ne'er ___ would flinch, they'd

like a rov - ing | sign, And the | peo - ple all say, "There
nev - er fret or | whine; Like ___ | good ___ old bricks They

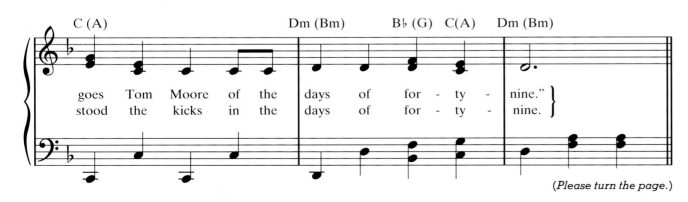

goes Tom Moore of the | days of for - ty - | nine."
stood the kicks in the | days of for - ty - | nine.

(*Please turn the page.*)

Additional verses:

3. There was old Lame Jess, a hard old
     cuss, who never did repent.
   He never was known to miss a drink
     nor to ever spend a cent.
   But old Lame Jess, like all the rest,
     to death he did resign,
   And in his bloom went up the flume
     in the days of forty-nine.
   (*Chorus*)

4. There was Poker Bill, one of the boys,
     who was always in for a game;
   Whether he lost or whether he won,
     to him it was all the same.
   He would ante up and draw his cards,
     he would go a hatful blind.
   In the game of death, Bill lost his
     breath in the days of forty-nine.
   (*Chorus*)

5. There was New York Jake, the butcher
     boy, he was always getting tight,
   And every time that he'd get full
     he was spoiling for a fight;
   But Jake rampaged against a knife
     in the hands of old Bob Pine,
   And over Jake they held a wake
     in the days of forty-nine.
   (*Chorus*)

6. There was Ragshag Bill from Buffalo,
     I never will forget,
   He would roar all day and he'd roar all
     night and I guess he's roaring yet.
   One night he fell in a prospect hole
     in a roaring bad design,
   And in that hole he roared out his soul
     in the days of forty-nine.
   (*Chorus*)

7. Of all the comrades that I've had
     there's none that's left to boast,
   And I'm left alone in my misery
     like some poor wandering ghost;
   And as I pass from town to town
     they call me the rambling sign,
   "There goes Tom Moore, a bummer
     shore, of the days of forty-nine."
   (*Chorus*)

THE DAYS OF '49 *(Continued)*

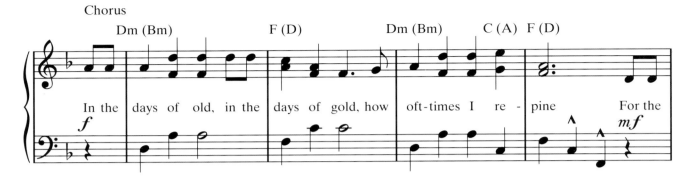

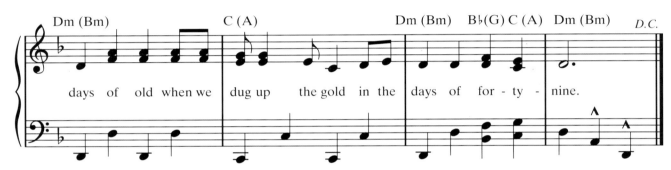

In the days of old, in the days of gold, how oft-times I re-pine For the days of old when we dug up the gold in the days of for-ty - nine.

In an era when the average laborer earned no more than a dollar a day, a few dollars would not have been such a bad return. But the prospectors had to contend with wildly inflated prices for the most common goods—a 60-cent pan went for $16, potatoes were a dollar a pound, an egg cost 50 cents, a chicken $4, shirts could be laundered for $8 a dozen—and they lived in unspeakably squalid camps plagued by disease, crime, and loneliness. In the end, very few Forty-Niners struck it rich— except, of course, for those who made their living not from prospecting gold, but from "prospecting" the prospectors. Men like Collis P. Huntington, Charles Crocker, Mark Hopkins, Leland Stanford, and Samuel Brannon founded storybook fortunes on selling hardware, groceries, and other supplies—all at premium prices—to the men of '49.

The Forty-Niner
Emanuel Wyttenbach, American, 1857–1894
Advertisement for Seal Rock Tobacco Co.
Color lithograph
MMA

Forty-Niners Playing Cards
Emanuel Wyttenbach, American, 1857–1894
Lithograph, cigar box top
MMA

CAVALRY CHARGE

Cavalry Charge on the Southern Plains
Frederic Remington, American, 1861–1909
Oil on canvas, 1907
MMA

Frederic Remington's admiration of the U.S. cavalryman is evident in every one of his many paintings depicting the service. In fact, the forces that fought the Indian Wars from the end of the Civil War to the early 1890s were understaffed, undertrained, and underequipped. Yet the cavalry endured, and Remington helped transmute it into American legend and lore.

Briskly

Few western subjects stir up such powerful and conflicting emotions as the buffalo. Mid–nineteenth-century travelers described herds so vast that they actually blackened the seemingly endless plains. Within the space of two or three decades, though, the buffalo had been hunted nearly to extinction.

The culture of the Plains Indians revolved around the great buffalo herds. The animals were a source of meat, clothing (buffalo robes), and shelter (tanned hides made good teepees). The hunt not only demanded and developed the extraordinary horsemanship for which the Indians of the plains were famed, it also helped hold together the loosely organized, nomadic tribes. Buffalo hunting was an art and a ritual that required courage, endurance, and closely coordinated effort from the men and a sophisticated level of organization and cooperation from the women, who had to care for the meat and prepare the hides.

Buffalo hide coat
American, ca. 1875
BBHC

24

THE BUFFALO HUNTERS

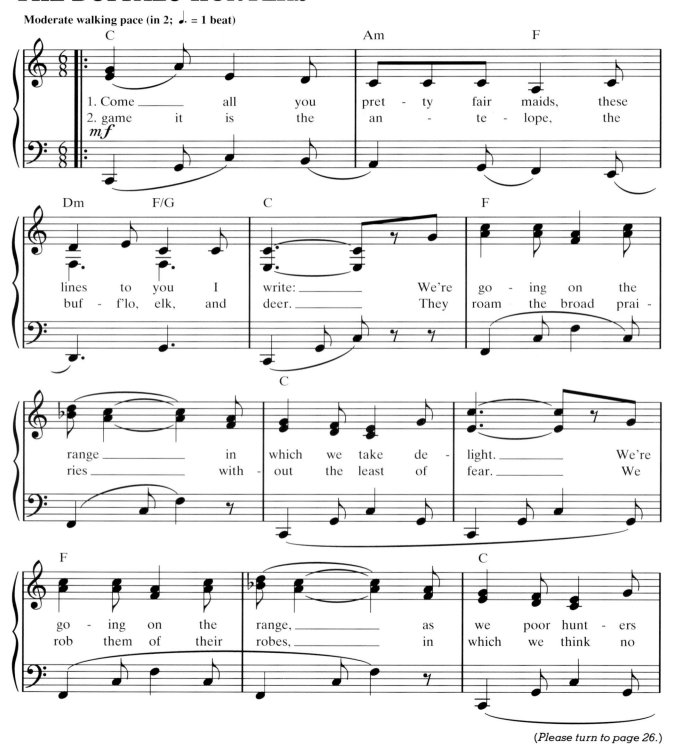

Moderate walking pace (in 2; ♩. = 1 beat)

1. Come _____ all you pret - ty fair maids, these
2. game it is the an - te - lope, the

lines to you I write: _____ We're go - ing on the
buf - f'lo, elk, and deer. _____ They roam the broad prai -

range _____ in which we take de - light. _____ We're
ries _____ with - out the least of fear. _____ We

go - ing on the range, _____ as we poor hunt - ers
rob them of their robes, _____ in which we think no

(*Please turn to page 26.*)

Last of the Buffalo
Albert Bierstadt, American, 1830–1902
Oil on canvas, ca. 1888
BBHC

Historians are fond of pointing out that it was not the U.S. Cavalry but the destruction of the buffalo that drove the Indians from the plains. At first, white fur traders and travelers, like the Indians themselves, hunted only what they needed for meat and clothing. The gold rush of 1849, however, greatly increased the demand for buffalo meat and hides, as did each of the white man's successive western enterprises. Buffalo meat fed the emigrant wagon trains and fueled the muscle that built the transcontinental railroads.

Although he had been an intrepid Pony Express rider and a great army scout, William Cody earned his mythic stature and his nickname—Buffalo Bill—from the hunting he did supplying meat under contract to the Union Pacific Railroad. This fact is important, because it shows us what the buffalo hunt had come to mean to white America.

As the lyrics of the song suggest, buffalo hunting had become a test of manly endurance, skill, and courage. And once that happened, the ordinary laws of supply and demand no longer applied. The plains swarmed with young white hunters, itching to prove themselves by slaughtering far more of the animals than could ever be used. The government abetted them by paying bounties on the hides, while the rancher and the sodbuster—at deadly odds about most other things— agreed in welcoming the extermination of these herds, which usurped good range land and interfered with farming.

A way of life, a rite of passage, an infernal obstacle, a shameful tragedy, the buffalo represented many things to the many people of the West.

THE BUFFALO HUNTERS *(Continued)*

Buffalo Bill's Wild West
Back cover of a pamphlet for
Buffalo Bill's Wild West Show
Color lithograph, 1885   MMA

Additional verses:

3. The buffalo is the largest and the noblest of the band.
   He sometimes refuses to throw us up his hand.
   With shaggy mane thrown forward, and head raised to the sky,
   He seems to say "We're coming, boys, so hunter, mind your eye!"

4. It's all of the day long as we go tramping 'round
   In search of the buff'lo that we may shoot him down;
   Our guns upon our shoulders, our belts of forty rounds,
   We send them up Salt River to their happy hunting grounds.

5. Our houses are made of buffalo hides, we build them tall and round;
   Our fires are made of buffalo chips, our beds are on the ground.
   Our furniture is the camp kettle, the coffee pot, and pan,
   Our chuck is buffalo beef and bread intermingled well with sand.

TENTING ON THE OLD CAMPGROUND

Composed during the Civil War, this poignant song remained popular long afterward, especially in wartime. It also found a special place in the heart of William Frederick "Buffalo Bill" Cody, quite possibly the most famous westerner of all time. Buffalo Bill's renown was no accident, for this natural-born showman tirelessly engineered it. This is not to say, though, that he was anything less than the authentic article. Born in Scott County, Iowa, in 1846, Cody moved with his family to the newly opened Kansas Territory in 1854 and, upon his father's death three years later, went to work for the freighting firm of Majors & Russell (later Russell, Majors & Waddell) as a mounted messenger. This experience made him an obvious candidate for William H. Russell's Pony Express, which the fourteen-year-old Cody joined in 1860.

He went on to service with the Seventh Kansas Volunteer Cavalry during the Civil War, where he perhaps learned this song, and then served with distinction as an army scout during the Indian Wars.

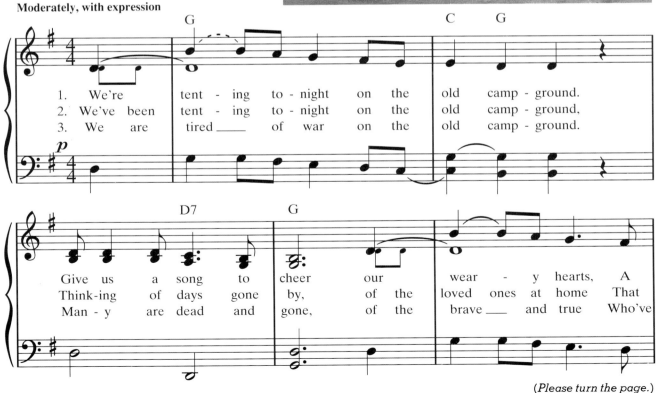

1. We're tent - ing to - night on the old camp - ground.
2. We've been tent - ing to - night on the old camp - ground,
3. We are tired of war on the old camp - ground.

Give us a song to cheer our wear - y hearts, A
Think - ing of days gone by, of the loved ones at home That
Man - y are dead and gone, of the brave and true Who've

Colonel William F. Cody
Rosa Bonheur, French, 1822–1899
Oil on canvas, 1889
BBHC

(Please turn the page.)

27

A popular dime novelist of the period, Ned Buntline, made Buffalo Bill the hero of a book he later dramatized, with Buffalo Bill and Wild Bill Hickok playing themselves, and soon a number of biographies appeared. In 1883, Buffalo Bill capitalized on his fame by starting a tremendously successful touring Wild West Show, which featured such notables as Buck Taylor ("King of the Cowboys"), Annie Oakley ("Little Sure Shot"), and Chief Sitting Bull.

Buffalo Bill's Wild West
Cover of a pamphlet for Buffalo Bill's Wild West Show
Color lithograph, 1885   MMA

TENTING ON THE OLD CAMPGROUND *(Continued)*

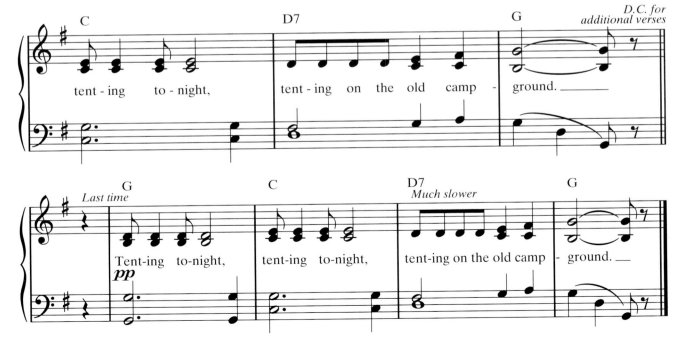

tent - ing   to - night,   tent - ing   on   the   old   camp - ground. ____

D.C. for additional verses

Last time

pp

Tent-ing   to-night,   tent-ing   to-night,   *Much slower*   tent-ing on the old camp - ground. ___

The great American painter Winslow Homer was closely associated with the landscape of the Atlantic coast rather than with the American West. However, he did a great deal of work as a magazine illustrator during the Civil War, and *Rainy Day in Camp*, completed six years after the surrender at Appomattox, effectively evokes the melancholy atmosphere of the ever-makeshift life of soldiers at the front.

A Rainy Day in Camp
Winslow Homer, American, 1836–1910
Oil on canvas, 1871
MMA

SWEET BETSY FROM PIKE

When we think of adventure in the early West we usually picture trappers, traders, soldiers, warriors, cowboys, and prospectors. We think of solitary men, wifeless and childless. This song, first popular in the gold rush era of 1849–59, may have been born of simple loneliness. During this period, women constituted a meager eight percent of California's population, and one gold camp entrepreneur actually offered a peek at a lady's bonnet and boots for the admission price of one dollar.

But there is more to this song and more to W.H.D. Koerner's *Madonna of the Prairie*, painted as an illustration to a popular western novel by Emerson Hough. While many songs and paintings depict the conquest of the West, "Sweet Betsy" and *Madonna of the Prairie* celebrate the civilizing of the West represented by the new breed of settlers who came after the lone trapper and trader, the prospector out for instant wealth, and the bachelor cowboy. The new settlers were families, who brought no lust for sudden riches, no aspirations to build empires, no hankering after a lawless life. They brought instead a desire for the civilization and stability all families need to prosper. Solitary men may have opened the West, but it was civilized by "madonnas" like Sweet Betsy, braving the privations of frontier existence, forsaking the safe eastern life to nurture a family in the new, uncertain, but hopeful American West.

Madonna of the Prairie
W.H.D. Koerner,
American, 1878–1938
Oil on canvas, 1921   BBHC

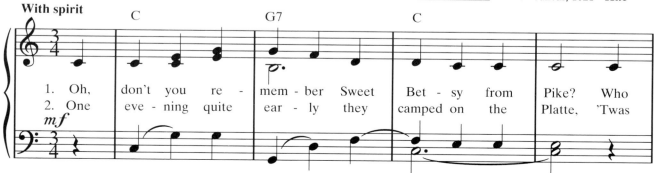

With spirit

1. Oh, don't you re - mem - ber Sweet Bet - sy from the Pike? Who
2. One eve - ning quite ear - ly they camped on the Platte, 'Twas

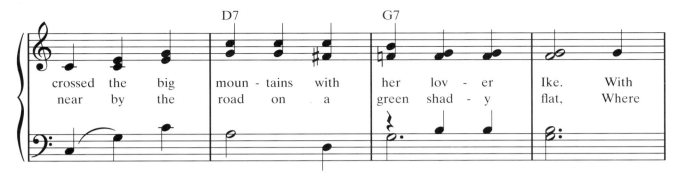

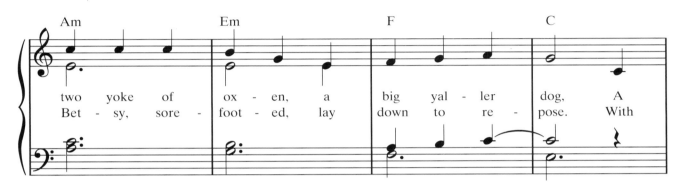

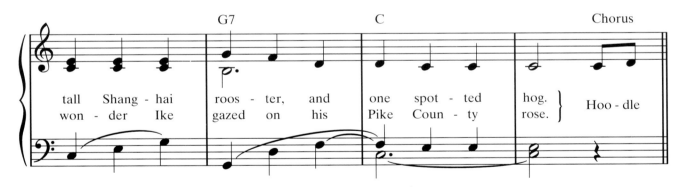

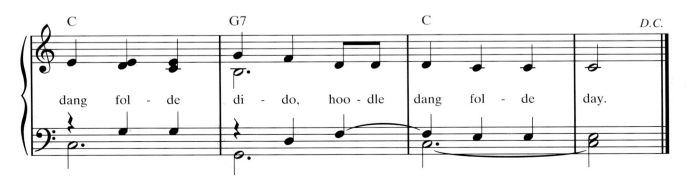

crossed the big / near by the mountains with / road on a her lov-er / green shad-y Ike. / flat, With / Where

two yoke of / Bet-sy, sore- oxen, a / foot-ed, lay big yal-ler / down to re- dog, / pose. A / With

tall Shang-hai / won-der Ike roos-ter, and / gazed on his one spot-ted / Pike Coun-ty hog. / rose. } Hoo-dle

dang fol-de di-do, hoo-dle dang fol-de day.

Additional verses:

3. The Shanghai ran off,
   and their cattle all died.
   That morning the last
   piece of bacon was fried.
   Poor Ike was discouraged
   and Betsy got mad.
   The dog drooped his tail
   and looked wondrously sad.
   (Chorus)

4. They soon reached the desert
   where Betsy gave out,
   And down in the sand
   she lay rolling about,
   While Ike half distracted
   looked on with surprise,
   Saying, "Betsy, get up,
   you'll get sand in your eyes."
   (Chorus)

5. Sweet Betsy got up
   in a great deal of pain,
   Declared she'd go back
   to Pike County again;
   But Ike gave a sigh,
   and they fondly embraced,
   And they traveled along
   with his arm round her waist.
   (Chorus)

6. *Repeat first verse and Chorus.*

Buff Cochin China Cock
Card from "Fifty Prize and Game Chickens"
series, published by Allen & Ginter,
American Tobacco Co., Richmond, Virginia
Color lithograph, late 19th century MMA

BURY ME NOT ON THE LONE PRAIRIE

The great eminences and depressions of the western landscape—its towering mountains and bottomless canyons—have been recorded in painting after painting. Western travelers, however, were often even more impressed by the vast western prairie lands, which extend from Indiana to the slopes of the Rockies and the deserts of the Southwest: an ocean of man-tall grass navigated by covered wagons called prairie schooners.

If a man died along this long, lonely way, well, that is where he had to be laid to rest—far from the familiar green hillsides of the East. Hundreds of thousands of men, women, and children traversed the prairie on their journey west, and, certainly, many died. Indians killed a few; bandits, fewer still. Remorseless sun or unrelenting cold killed far more. But the greatest killer was invisible: disease, chiefly cholera and dysentery. These were the two plagues of trail and camp life, for sanitary practices were poor, food was bad and scarce, and the path was hard and exhausting.

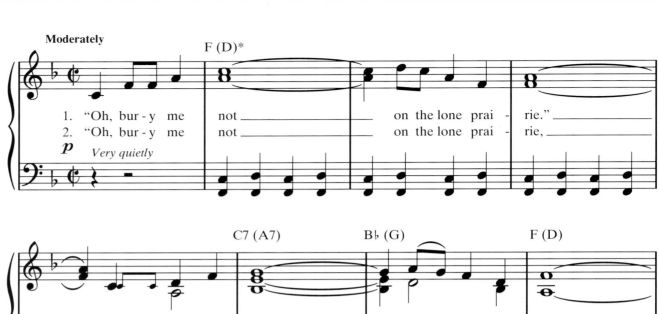

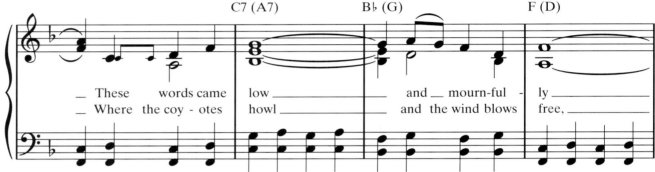

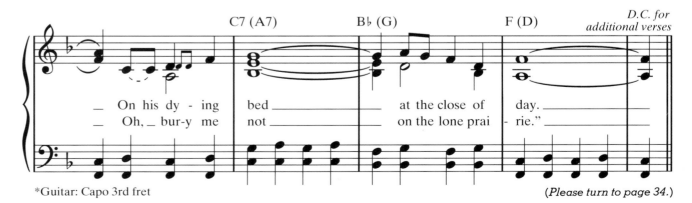

*Guitar: Capo 3rd fret

(*Please turn to page 34.*)

Vultures on a Tree
Antoine Louis Barye, French, 1796–1875
Watercolor and gouache
MMA

For many who made the trek, perhaps even for most who did, the West was a land of hope and of hope fulfilled. But, as this grim song attests, those who rode toward the dying sun might reach their final destination long before they wished to.

Death meant life for some denizens of the prairie. Both the vulture and the coyote feed mainly on carrion, which means they occupy an important niche in prairie ecology, but one that is distasteful to most people.

BURY ME NOT ON THE LONE PRAIRIE *(Continued)*

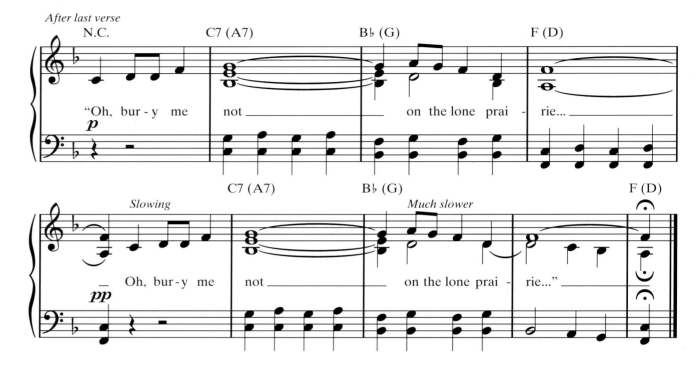

The photographer Charles Belden, a chronicler of cowboy life, actually adopted a coyote as a pet. Belden posed him next to a tombstone, took the photo, added the verse, and then rephotographed the print.

Additional verses:

3. "It matters not, often I've been told,
   Where the body lies when the heart grows cold.
   Yet grant, oh grant, this wish to me:
   Oh, bury me not on the lone prairie."

4. "I've always wished to be laid when I died
   In the little churchyard on the green hillside.
   By my father's grave there let mine be,
   And bury me not on the lone prairie."

5. "Let my death sleep be where my mother's pray'r
   And a sister's tear will mingle there.
   Where friends can come and weep o'er me.
   Oh, bury me not on the lone prairie."

6. "Oh, bury me not on the lone prairie,
   Where the wolves can howl and growl o'er me.
   Fling a handful of roses o'er my grave,
   With a pray'r to Him who my soul will save."

7. "Oh, bury me not..." and his voice failed there,
   But we took no heed of his dying pray'r.
   In a narrow grave, just six by three,
   We buried him there on the lone prairie.

8. And cowboys now as they roam the plain,
   For they marked the spot where his bones were lain,
   Fling a handful of roses o'er his grave
   With a pray'r to God, his soul to save.

PATSY ORY ORY AYE

The frontier West had plenty to offer, but what it offered in the greatest abundance was distance, and distance demanded travel. Where there were rivers, there were flatboats and steamboats. Overland, first came the wagons, then the stagecoaches, and, finally, the railroads. Railroads required muscle to build them, and that muscle had to be cheap. Two immigrant groups were particularly exploited for the purpose: the Irish (from whom this song comes) and the Chinese. Irish laborers fled a homeland plagued by famine, a wretched economy, and political oppression. Often treated contemptuously on their arrival in America, they were put to the kind of work less desperate groups declined, such as wielding a sledgehammer all day.

Chinese first began working on the railroad in 1865. James Harvey Strobridge, chief of staff for the Central Pacific, was racing to complete the transcontinental railroad, and facing an acute labor shortage he began reluctantly hiring Chinese hands. They soon proved themselves extraordinary workers, and Strobridge began "importing" them direct from China. The print reproduced here, illustrating the driving of the golden spike that joined the Central Pacific and Union Pacific rail lines at Promontory Point, Utah, on May 10, 1869, includes a single Chinese worker to represent the many who labored on the railroad.

Driving the Golden Spike at Promontory Point to Complete the Transcontinental Railroad After Filippo Costaggini, American, 1837–1907, from his frieze for the U.S. Capitol dome Commercial printing process, ca. 1890 MMA

Moderately

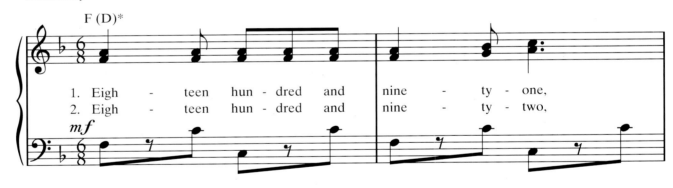

1. Eigh - teen hun - dred and nine - ty - one,
2. Eigh - teen hun - dred and nine - ty - two,

That's __ the year that I ____ be - gun, That's __ the year that
Look - ing a - round for some-thing to do, Look - ing a - round for

*Guitar: Capo 3rd fret

(*Please turn the page.*)

35

The ceremony, by the way, did not go smoothly. Chinese workmen, apparently all too aware of how Caucasians felt about them, were lowering the last rail into place when a photographer hollered, "Shoot!" They dropped the five-hundred-pound rail and ran. Leland Stanford, one of the principal financiers of the transcontinental railroad, prepared to drive the golden spike, which was wired (as the print shows) to the telegraph line so that each blow would be transmitted across the nation. He swung, and he missed. With an assist from workers—who had had a continent's worth of practice—the spike was finally driven home.

Man with a Sledge Hammer
Mahonri Young, American, 1877–1957
Charcoal and pastel on paper, 1903
MMA

D. & R. G. Locomotive
Edward Hopper, American, 1882–1967
Watercolor and pencil on paper, 1925
MMA

PATSY ORY ORY AYE *(Continued)*

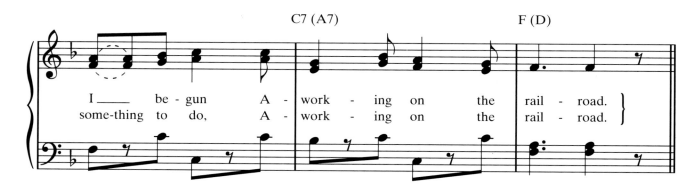

I ____ be-gun A - work - ing on the rail - road.
some-thing to do, A - work - ing on the rail - road.

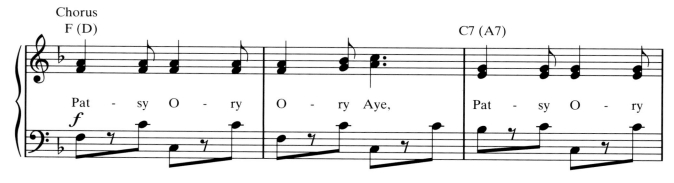

Chorus
Pat - sy O - ry O - ry Aye, Pat - sy O - ry

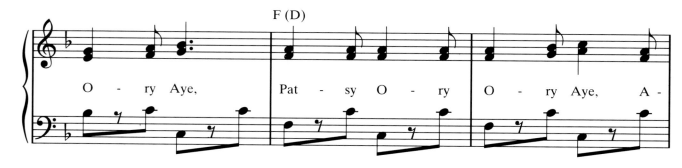

O - ry Aye, Pat - sy O - ry O - ry Aye, A-

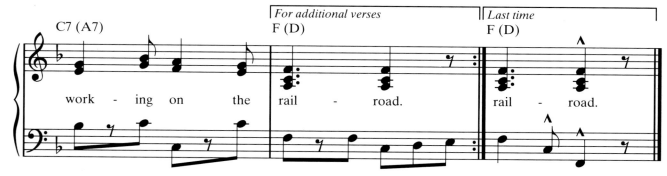

work - ing on the rail - road. rail - road.

Additional verses:

3.
Eighteen hundred and ninety-three,
Section boss a-driving me,
Section boss a-driving me,
A-working on the railroad. *(Chorus)*

4.
Eighteen hundred and ninety-four,
Hands and feet were getting sore,
Hands and feet were getting sore,
A-working on the railroad. *(Chorus)*

5.
Eighteen hundred and ninety-five,
Found myself more dead than alive,
Found myself more dead than alive,
A-working on the railroad. *(Chorus)*

6.
Eighteen hundred and ninety-six,
Kicked a couple of dynamite sticks,
Kicked a couple of dynamite sticks,
A-working on the railroad. *(Chorus)*

7.
Eighteen hundred and ninety-seven,
Found myself on the road to heaven,
Found myself on the road to heaven,
A-working on the railroad. *(Chorus)*

8.
Eighteen hundred and ninety-eight,
A-picking the lock in the pearly gate,
A-picking the lock in the pearly gate,
A-working on the railroad. *(Chorus)*

9.
Eighteen hundred and ninety-nine,
I found the angels drinking wine,
They gave me a harp and a crown divine,
Overlooking the railroad. *(Chorus)*

10.
Eighteen hundred and ninety-ten,
Found myself on the earth again,
Found myself on the earth again,
A-working on the railroad. *(Chorus)*

THE TEXAS RANGERS

Today a small, elite group of highly trained investigative law-enforcement officials, the Texas Rangers were organized by the colonist and entrepreneur Stephen F. Austin in 1826, when Texas was still a province of Mexico. Their mission during this early period was chiefly to engage hostile Indians and suppress raiding, but in 1836, with the outbreak of the Texas Revolution, they also protected settlers against Mexican marauders. During the Mexican-American War of 1846–47, they served with Generals Zachary Taylor and Winfield Scott. Following this war and the Civil War, their duties increasingly involved law enforcement—a difficult task on the unruly Texas frontier.

Charles Schreyvogel's painting *My Bunkie* actually depicts U.S. cavalrymen, but the exciting action matches the drama of this song about a fight between the Texas Rangers and a band of fierce Indians. Schreyvogel, who painted some of the most vivid scenes of western life—especially cavalry subjects—was not born in the wide-open spaces of the West, but in the crowded slums of New York's Lower East Side. He held a number of jobs until friends raised enough money to finance his art training in Europe. When he returned to New York in 1890, he painted portraits and landscapes, but without financial success.

The Cheyenne
Frederic Remington, American, 1861–1909
Bronze; 1902, this cast 1907
MMA

Moderately

1. Come all you Tex-as Ran-gers, wher-ev-er you may be, I'll tell you of some trou-ble that hap-pened un-to me. My name is noth-ing

2. When at the age of six-teen I joined this jol-ly band, We marched from San An-to-nio down to the Ri-o Grande. Our cap-tain he in-

*Guitar: Capo 3rd fret

(Please turn to page 40.)

My Bunkie
Charles Schreyvogel, American, 1861–1912
Oil on canvas MMA

In 1893, Schreyvogel painted some of the stars of Buffalo Bill's Wild West Show, which was touring New York City. He earned enough money to take a trip out west, where he made studies of Indians, cowboys, and cavalry life, eventually becoming a successful western artist and illustrator.

The revolver pictured here was used by the early Texas Rangers during the period of border disputes that followed the Texas Revolution. Designed by master gunsmith Samuel Colt in 1836, it was dubbed the Paterson because it was manufactured in Paterson, New Jersey. A five-shooter, it is a primitive-looking ancestor of the more famous six-shooters Colt's company produced later in the century. The best known of these are the .31-caliber 1849 model (the most popular pocket revolver in the world, from its introduction in 1849 to the 1870s), the .36-caliber Navy Model of 1851, the .44-caliber Army Model of 1860, and the .45-caliber Colt Peacemaker, introduced in 1873. It was this last long-barreled revolver— also known simply as the Colt .45 —that was the weapon of choice for many a gunfighter.

Colt Paterson percussion revolver
Designed by Samuel Colt, American, 1814–1862
Steel, ivory, silver; ca. 1838–40   MMA

THE TEXAS RANGERS (Continued)

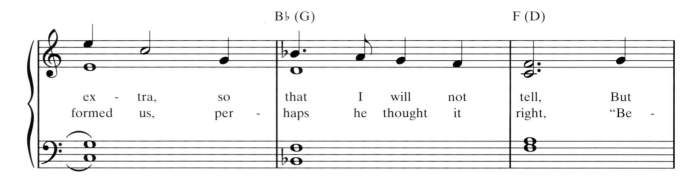

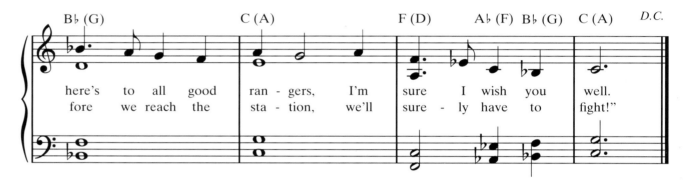

Additional verses:

3.
I saw the smoke ascending, it seemed to reach the sky.
The first thought then came to me, "My time has come to die!"
And when the bugles sounded, our captain gave command,
"To arms, to arms," he shouted, "and by your horses stand."

4.
I saw the Indians coming, I heard their awful yell.
My feelings at the moment, no human tongue can tell.
I saw their glittering lances, their arrows around me flew,
Till all my strength had left me, and all my courage too.

5.
We fought for five full hours before the strife was o'er.
The likes of dead and wounded, I've never seen before.
And when the sun had risen, the Indians they had fled.
We loaded up our rifles and counted up our dead.

6.
Now all of us were wounded, our noble captain slain.
And when the sun was shining across the bloody plain,
Six of the noblest rangers that ever roamed the West,
Were buried by their comrades with arrows in their breasts.

7.
Perhaps you have a mother, likewise a sister too.
Perhaps you have a sweetheart, to weep and mourn for you.
If this be your position, although you'd like to roam,
I'll tell you from experience, you'd better stay at home.

THE YELLOW ROSE OF TEXAS

The Yellow Rose of Texas is not a flower, but a person, a servant named Emily D. West, who was indentured to Colonel James Morgan, who fought in the war for the independence of Texas from Mexico.

Girl with Roses
Probably by Paul Wyttenbach, American, active 1900–1920
Color lithograph, published by Cosmopolitan Lithograph Co., 1912
MMA

Briskly

1. There's a yel-low rose of Tex-as I'm go-in' for to see, No
2. Where the Ri - o Grande is flow-ing and star-ry skies are bright, She
3. Oh, __ now I'm goin' to find her, my heart is full of woe; We'll

oth - er sol - dier knows her, no - bod-y on - ly me. She
walks a - long the riv - er in the qui - et sum - mer night. She
sing the song to-geth-er we sang so long a - go. We'll

cried so when I left her, it like to broke my heart, And
thinks if I re - mem - ber we part - ed long a - go; I
play the ban - jo gai - ly and sing the songs of yore, And the

if I ev - er find her, we nev - er-more will part.
prom-ised to come back a - gain and nev - er let her go.
yel - low rose of Tex - as will be mine for - ev - er-more.

(*Please turn the page.*)

Emily was at Morgan's plantation seventeen miles southeast of present-day Houston when the Mexican army, under General Antonio López de Santa Anna, took possession of it. (Morgan was commanding Texas forces on Galveston Island at the time.)

On the morning of April 21, 1836, Sam Houston, in command of the Texas revolutionaries, climbed a tree and watched Emily serve Santa Anna his breakfast. The Mexican dictator had a well-known weakness for pretty women, and Houston remarked that he hoped the girl would keep Santa Anna occupied all day. The Texans attacked that afternoon — while Santa Anna was, in fact, with Emily. The spectacle of a commanding general frantically running about in his red slippers was not a sight calculated to rally his troops, and the decisive Battle of San Jacinto was over in less than twenty minutes, the Texans having surprised and defeated a force more than twice their size. This song, commemorating Emily D. West's peculiar and peculiarly interesting role in the battle, appeared shortly after the Texas Revolution and remained a favorite with soldiers, cowboys, and others who had left sweethearts behind.

THE YELLOW ROSE OF TEXAS (Continued)

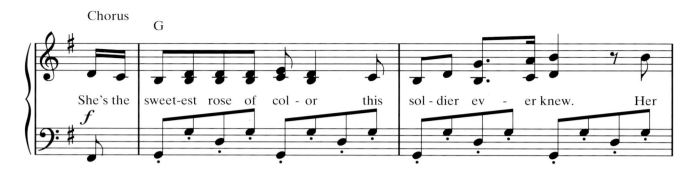

She's the sweet-est rose of col - or this sol - dier ev - er knew. Her

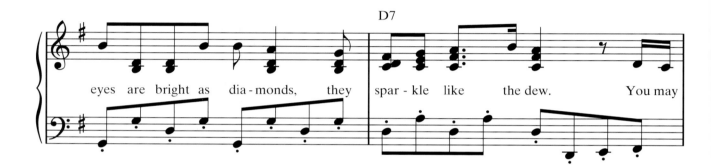

eyes are bright as dia - monds, they spar - kle like the dew. You may

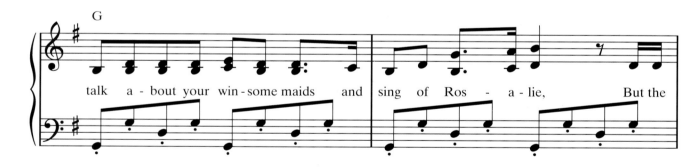

talk a - bout your win - some maids and sing of Ros - a - lie, But the

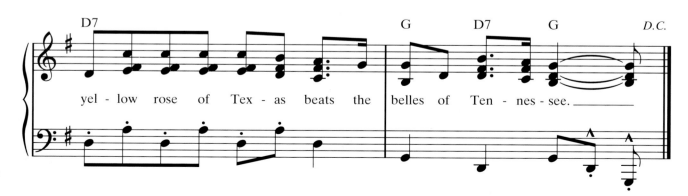

yel - low rose of Tex - as beats the belles of Ten - nes - see.

"We Been Missing You Something Frightful," He Said.
W.H.D. Koerner, American, 1878–1938
Oil on canvas, 1925 BBHC

GIT ALONG, LITTLE DOGIES

The best-loved western song of them all, "Git Along, Little Dogies" is a marvelous capsule history of cattle raising, the business that created the cowboy. The first verse is a snapshot of the cowboy himself, and three details tell it all. He rides along—doesn't gallop, doesn't canter, doesn't trot—he wears his hat (you never see a cowboy without his hat) just so, "throwed back" with a studied casualness all his own, and he allows himself a single extravagance in fancy spurs equipped with jinglebobs. The jingle-jangle of these ornaments proclaims the cowboy's coming to anyone within hearing and keeps him company during long days and nights of often solitary work. Some cowboys say the music of the jinglebobs serves to keep the cattle calm.

In the 1870s and 1880s, tough Longhorn cattle (half-ton monsters the cowboys called with wary affection "little dogies"), were raised "way down in Texas" and exported to many parts of the United States. How do you export anywhere from 500 to 5,000 head of cattle at a time? In a herd, on the hoof.

Stray Man Heads Home
W.H.D. Koerner, American, 1878–1938
Oil on canvas, 1928
BBHC

Flowing

F (D)*   Bb (G)   F (D)

1. As I was a-walk-ing one morn-ing for plea-sure, I
2. It's ear-ly in spring that we round up the do-gies, We

p

G7 (E7)   C7 (A7)   F (D)

spied a cow-punch-er a-rid-in' a-long. His hat was throwed back and his
mark them and brand them and bob off their tails. We round up our hors-es, load

*Guitar: Capo 3rd fret

spurs were a - jing - lin', And as he ap-proached he was sing - in' this song:
up the chuck wag - on, And then throw the do - gies out on - to the trail.

Chorus

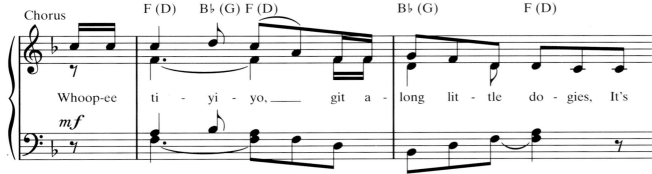

Whoop-ee ti - yi - yo, _____ git a - long lit - tle do - gies, It's

mf

your mis - for - tune and none of my own. Whoop-ee ti - yi - yo, _____ git a -

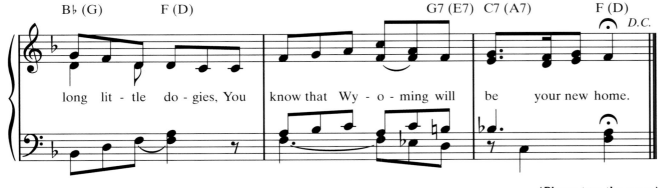

long lit - tle do - gies, You know that Wy - o - ming will be your new home.

D.C.

(*Please turn the page.*)

Additional verses:

3. It's whooping and yelling
 and drivin' the dogies
 And oh how I wish
 you would only go on!
 It's whooping and punching,
 go on, little dogies,
 You know that Wyoming
 will be your new home.
 (*Chorus*)

4. Some boys, they go up on
 the trail just for pleasure,
 But that's where they get it
 most awfully wrong.
 You haven't a notion
 the trouble they give us,
 It takes all our time
 to keep moving along.
 (*Chorus*)

5. Your mother was raised
 way down in Texas,
 Where the jimson weed
 and the sandburs grow.
 We'll fill you up
 on prickly pear and cholla,
 Then throw you on
 the trail to Idaho.
 (*Chorus*)

Engraved spurs
American, ca. 1925
Leather, chrome, and silver
BBHC

45

GIT ALONG, LITTLE DOGIES *(Continued)*

The cowboy's hard job began with the spring roundup (the original sense of the word rodeo), in which yearlings and two-year-olds were culled from a ranchman's entire free-ranging herd, marked for shipment, branded to identify them as the property of a particular outfit — ranch or cattle company — and set out on the long trail north. The song makes it all seem pretty fast; actually, the roundup might take several weeks, and the trail drive could consume three or four months. At the rate of ten or twelve miles per day, the distance between Texas and Wyoming, the destination for the cattle in this song, is very great.

A history of the cattle trade, this song is also a livestock lullaby, sung by the cowboy in soothing cadence with his jinglebobs to help him keep 'em moving along the trail.

Above the Sea of Round, Shiny Backs the Thin Loops Swirled and Shot into Volumes of Dust
N. C. Wyeth, American, 1882–1945
Oil on canvas, 1904–05   BBHC

CIELITO LINDO

The generations of easterners (and perhaps even some modern westerners) who grew up watching William S. Hart, Tom Mix, Gene Autry, Roy Rogers, and John Wayne in the movies and on television may find it difficult to see cowboys as anything other than blue-eyed men with names like McCoy, Murphy, and Jones. In fact, the pedigree of all cowboys—black, white, brown, red—is found not in the freedom of the plains but in the slavery of Spanish America.

El Ranchero
Hesiquio Iriarte, Mexican, 1820?–1897?
Lithograph from *Los Mexicanos pintados por sí mismos . . .*
Published by M. Murguía y Co., Mexico City, 1854
MMA

Brightly

A pronunciation guide for the Spanish lyrics appears in italics.

De la Sie - rra Mo - re - na, Cie - li - to
Day lah See-ay - rah Moe - ray - nah, See-ay - lee - toe

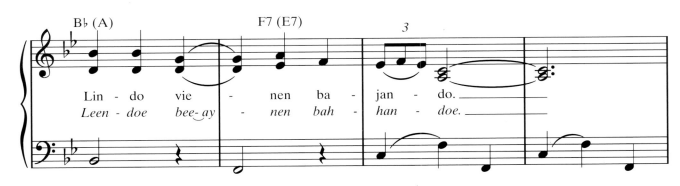

Lin - do vie - nen ba - jan - do.
Leen - doe bee-ay - nen bah - han - doe.

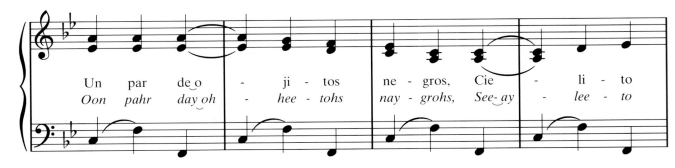

Un par de o - ji - tos ne - gros, Cie - li - to
Oon pahr day oh - hee - tohs nay - grohs, See-ay - lee - to

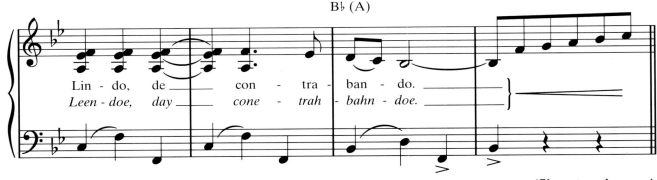

Lin - do, de con - tra - ban - do.
Leen - doe, day cone - trah - bahn - doe.

*Guitar: Capo 1st fret

(Please turn the page.)

47

When the cattle herds of the early Spanish missions had grown too large for the priests to manage, they trained mission Indians—who under Spanish colonial law were free, but for all practical purposes were enslaved to the mission and its surrounding ranchos—as horsemen. These early cowboys were called *vaqueros*—from the the Spanish word *vaca,* meaning "cow." To this day, a cowboy who likes to wear fancy duds and ornaments is called a buckaroo, which is how *vaquero* sounded to Anglo ears.

By the eighteenth century, most *vaqueros* were of mixed Indian and Spanish ancestry. They roped steers with a loop of braided rawhide called *la reata* (the later cowboy's lariat) and wore leather leggings, called *chaparreras* (chaps) to protect themselves from razor-sharp chaparral.

The "singing cowboy" of films and television could also trace his pedigree back to the Hispanic *vaquero.* While "Cielito Lindo," a traditional Spanish song, might have been too emotional for the stoic Anglo buckaroo, even he would have appreciated the message of its familiar chorus: "Sing and don't cry."

CIELITO LINDO *(Continued)*

Singing Vaquero
Emanuel Wyttenbach, American, 1857–1894
Brown and gray wash heightened with white
MMA

49

COWBOY JACK

He is America's knight: the cowboy—noble, brave, pure, and beholden to no one in a country untrammeled by the petty vagaries of politicians, plutocrats, and police. At least, that's the way Americans have always liked to see him. No one can deny that the cowboy's vocation required plenty of guts, endurance, and skill, but there is little romance about the motives that led most men to ride the range.

Many cowboys were discharged Confederate soldiers, who returned to a South so devastated by war that all opportunity had vanished. Despite the movie and television stereotypes, a great many cowboys were not Anglos, but Mexicans, Native Americans, and African Americans, poorest of the poor. The dirty, dangerous, lonely work of cowpunching was, for most men who undertook it, the only available means of making a living.

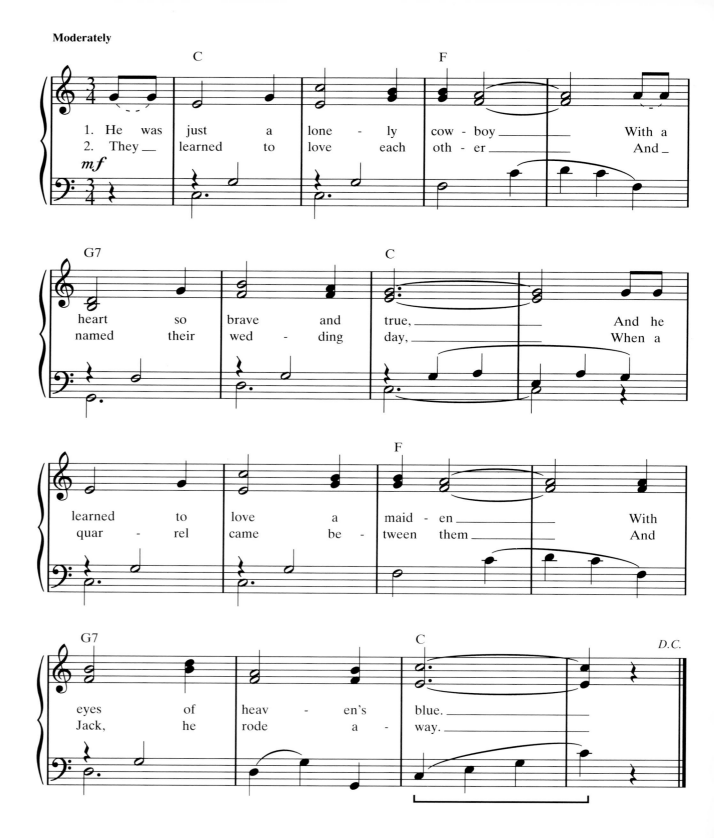

50

Cowboy at B. T. Ranch, North Dakota, 1887
Thomas Eakins, American, 1844–1916
Modern gelatin silver print
MMA

Cemetery, New Mexico
Marsden Hartley, American, 1877–1943
Oil on canvas, 1924
MMA

Additional verses:

3.
He joined a band of cowboys,
And tried to forget her name,
But out on the lonesome prairie
She waits for him the same.

4.
One night when work was finished,
Just at the close of day,
Someone said, "Sing a song, Jack,
To drive dull cares away."

5.
When Jack began his singing,
His mind did wander back,
For he sang of a maiden
Who waited for her Jack.

6.
"Your sweetheart waits for you, Jack;
Your sweetheart waits for you,
Out on the lonesome prairie
Where the skies are always blue."

7.
Jack left the camp next morning
Breathing his sweetheart's name.
"I'll go and ask forgiveness,
For I know that I'm to blame."

8.
But when he reached the prairie
He found a new-made mound.
And his friends they sadly told him
They'd laid his loved one down.

9.
They said as she lay dying
She breathed her sweetheart's name,
And asked them with her last breath
To tell him when he came:

10.
"Your sweetheart waits for you, Jack;
Your sweetheart waits for you,
Out on the lonesome prairie
Where the skies are always blue."

Women were a rarity in the cowboy's world, and a wife even rarer. No one wrote a ballad about a married cowboy, for he was "not the marrying kind." In popular songs—as, later, in popular films—a cowboy might fall in love, but he almost always rode away from the slightest promise of domestic bliss. Here the song-writer sends the lady to her grave, rather than imagine Cowboy Jack hitched. As the song correctly suggests, the cowboy bought his vaunted "freedom" at a heavy price. Rootless and propertyless, the rider of the range was often familyless as well. That was his blessing and his burden.

Like many modern American artists of the early twentieth century, Marsden Hartley was attracted to the desert Southwest, particularly the magnificent and austere landscape of New Mexico, which he visited in 1918 and 1919.

CINDY

Thomas Eakins, among the very greatest of America's realist painters, was a Phildelphian born and bred, but he was also an avid sportsman and horseman, who spent a rugged summer in the Badlands of North Dakota during 1887. He had a fine time there and indulged his realist's eye for detail in the colorful trappings of cowboy clothing and gear. Always a lover of music, Eakins developed a particular affection for cowboy tunes. Despite his feeling for the West, Eakins painted only a handful of western pictures. In 1892, some years after his single visit to the West, he dressed a friend in his cowboy clothes to model for this one.

While he posed, the friend strummed on a banjo, an instrument that grew up in the South, developing from African instruments familiar to the slaves. Forbidden to use loud instruments, these African Americans fashioned the quiet banjo, probably first using a gourd for a body and gut or fiber for strings. The instrument was popularized nationally by white entertainers who performed, both before and after the Civil War, in minstrel shows.

Cowboy Singing
Thomas Eakins, American, 1844–1916
Watercolor on paper
MMA

52

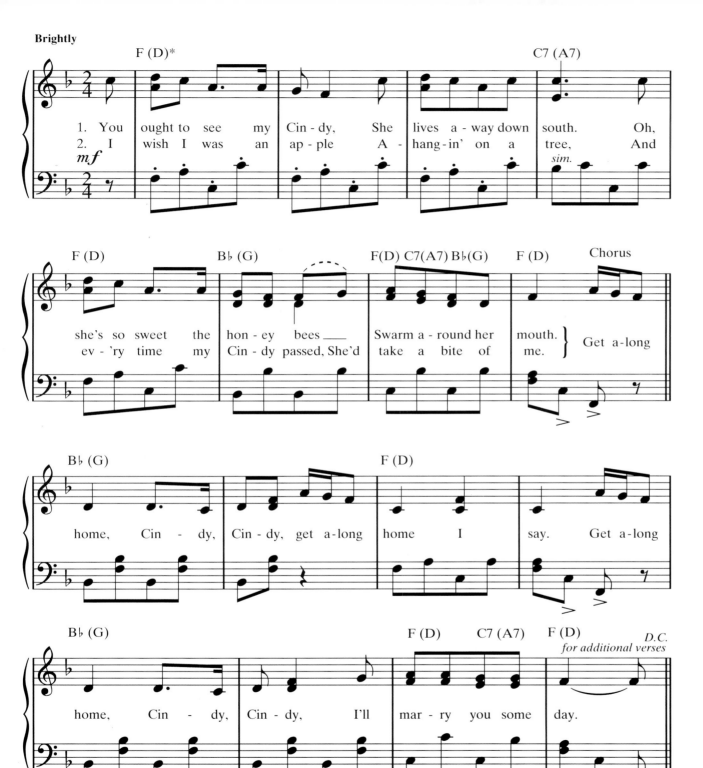

Additional verses:

3. She told me that she loved me,
   She called me "sugar plum,"
   She throwed her arms around me;
   I thought my time had come!
   (Chorus)

4. I wish I had a needle,
   As fine as I could sew,
   I'd sew that gal to my coattail
   And down the road I'd go.
   (Chorus)

5. Cindy in the springtime,
   Cindy in the fall,
   If I can't have my Cindy,
   I'll have no girl at all.
   (Chorus)

Tenor banjo
American, ca. 1900
Birch, ash, and various other materials
MMA

(Please turn the page.)

Not all songs sung in the West were about the West. Like the banjo, "Cindy" comes from the South—which is also the origin of many a genuine cowboy. When Texans went off to fight the Civil War, they let their livestock fend for themselves. By the end of the war, the result was millions of head of cattle ranging free across the state. With the economy of their native region in shambles and opportunities few and far between, a good many southern young men went west after Appomattox to round up Texas strays, brand them, and drive them to market up north. The young men brought with them few belongings, but those included the old songs they had learned and, in some cases, the banjos to play them on.

Marriage license for the City and
County of San Francisco
Emanuel Wyttenbach, American, 1857–1894
Lithograph with tint stone, 1870s
MMA

54

THE COWBOY

Eleanor Aveling, the daughter of Karl Marx, made this observation about the cowboy while touring the American West with her husband: "No class is harder worked, none so poorly paid for their services." It is in this spirit that the singer of our song laments his hard lot. He works all day, is lonely, owns virtually nothing, and sees as the sole reward of his labor the deathlike sleep of exhaustion.

Interestingly, the second verse suggests that, though this cowboy's life may be lacking in the amenities, he himself is not bereft of an education. The lines paraphrase a hopeful speech spoken in William Shakespeare's *As You Like It* (act 2, scene 1) by the wrongfully exiled Duke Senior:

Sweet are the uses of adversity,
Which like the toad, ugly
and venomous,
Wears yet a precious jewel
in his head;
And this our life, exempt from
public haunt,
Finds tongues in trees, books
in the running brooks,
Sermons in stones, and good
in every thing.

In other words, make the best of a bad situation. And such was the creed—spoken or unspoken—of many a cowboy.

Cowboy of the West
American
Color lithograph, published by
Clark's Thread, 1894   MMA

COWBOY OF THE WEST.
INDUSTRIAL SERIES.

1. All day on the prai-rie in a sad-dle I ride, Not
2. I wash in a pud-dle and wipe on a sack, I

e-ven a dog, boys, to trot by my side. My
car-ry my ward-robe a-long on my back. My

(Please turn the page.)

Frederic Remington, whose feeling for the strong character of the poorly equipped, underpaid, and hard-used cavalryman is evident in the painting reproduced with "Cavalry Charge," was equally attracted to the unflappable cowboy. The artist's *An Arizona Cowboy* is a colorful and romantic figure, to be sure, but he is, above all, real, his deftly sketched face suggesting a world of experience and a wealth of self-reliance.

An Arizona Cowboy
Frederic Remington, American, 1861–1909
Color lithograph from *A Bunch of Buckskins: Eight Drawings in Pastel by Frederic Remington,* published by R. H. Russell, New York, 1901   MMA

THE COWBOY (Continued)

fire I must kin - dle with chips gath - ered round, And
ceil - ing's the sky, _____ with my car - pet the grass, And My

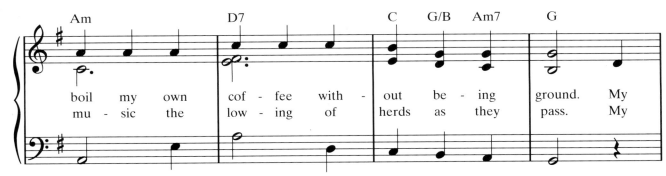

boil my own cof - fee with - out be - ing ground. My
mu - sic the low - ing of herds as they pass. My

bread lack - ing leav - en I bake in a pot, And I
books are the brooks, _ my ser - mons the stones, My _

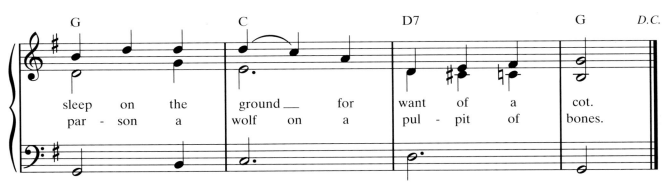

sleep on the ground _____ for want of a cot.
par - son a wolf on a pul - pit of bones.

Additional verses:

3. And then if my cooking
   is not too complete,
   No one can blame me
   for not wanting to eat.
   But show me a man that
   can sleep more profound
   Than the cowboy who stretches
   himself on the ground.
   My books teach me ever
   consistence to prize,
   My sermons, the small things
   I shall not despise.

4. My parson remarks
   from his pulpit of bones
   That the Lord favors those
   who look out for their own.
   But between me and love
   there's a gulf very wide,
   And some luckier fellow
   may call her his bride.
   My friends gently hint
   I am coming to grief,
   But men must make money
   and women have beef.

Vest
American, ca. 1935
Suede and leather
BBHC

Trail Herd to Wyoming
W.H.D. Koerner, American, 1878–1938
Oil on canvas, 1923
BBHC

THE OLD CHISHOLM TRAIL

With "Git Along, Little Dogies," "The Old Chisholm Trail" paints a vivid picture of the epic business of driving cattle. The Chisholm Trail was blazed as a wagon road by a frontier trader named Jesse Chisholm (1805–1868) and later developed by cattleman Joseph G. McCoy (1837–1915) as an avenue for the transportation of Texas Longhorns. It ran the 800 plus miles from Brownsville, Texas, to the Kansas railheads of Dodge City, Ellsworth, Abilene, and Junction City. The Chisholm was one of four principal cattle trails, along with the Shawnee (from Brownsville to Kansas City, Sedalia, and St. Louis, Missouri); the Western (from San Antonio, Texas, to Dodge City and then on to Fort Buford, at the fork of the Missouri and Yellowstone rivers, deep in Dakota Territory); and

the Goodnight-Loving (from the middle of Texas to Cheyenne, Wyoming).

Between 1866, when the legendary Texas cattlemen Oliver Loving and Charles Goodnight cut the trail named for them, and 1886–87, when a single terrible winter virtually wiped out the range-cattle industry, almost 100 million beeves and 10 million horses traversed these great trails. W. H. D.

Koerner had to make his *Trail Herd to Wyoming* a very wide painting to convey just what a mile-long column of 2,500 Longhorns (the average size of a trail herd) looked like. About ten cowboys, under the supervision of a trail boss, had charge of all these animals, as well as a saddle band of fifty to a hundred horses. The drive consumed three to four months, for which a cowboy earned

about a hundred dollars—which, charged against expenses, might well end up putting him "in the hole." Almost as long as the column of cattle and the days on the trail is this folk song about them. At least 143 stanzas are known to have been sung at one time or other.

(*Please turn the page.*)

Additional verses:
(Repeat Chorus after each verse)

3. I'm up in the morning before daylight;
   Before I sleep the moon shines bright.

4. Oh, it's bacon and beans most every day;
   We'll soon be eating this prairie hay.

5. With my seat in the saddle
   and my hand on the horn,
   I'm the best cowpuncher
   that ever was born.

6. No chaps, no slicker,
   and it's pourin' down rain;
   I swear I'll never night-herd again.

7. A stray in the herd
   and the boss said, "Kill it!"
   So I shot it in the rump
   with the handle of a skillet.

8. I went to the boss to draw my roll,
   And he had me figured out
   nine dollars in the hole.

9. Me and my boss we had a little spat,
   So I hit him in the face
   with my ten-gallon hat.

10. I'm going to sell my horse,
    going to sell my saddle,
    'Cause I'm tired of punching
    these Longhorn cattle.

11. With my knees in the saddle
    and my seat in the sky,
    I'll quit punchin' cows
    in the sweet by-and-by.

*Guitar: Capo 3rd fret

Cowboy boots
Justin's, Forth Worth, Texas, est. 1879
Tooled leather BBHC

THE BIG CORRAL

Not all cowboy songs come from anonymous range riders of the nineteenth century. This one was invented in 1922 by a folksinger named Romaine Lowdermilk, who, with two friends, premiered it at a local talent show in Wickenburg, Arizona. It was really a joke. Set to a gospel tune, "Press Along to Glory Land," it lampoons trail-drive "chuck" (i.e., cowhand cuisine) in its verses, while the chorus exhorts aspirations to a cowboy version of heaven: that Big Corral.

Moderately

1. That chuck - wag - on brute from the cat - tle chute,
2. Well, ear - ly in the morn - in' 'bout __ half - past four,

Press a - long to the Big Cor - ral.

He should be brand - ed
You'll hear him o - pen his

on the snoot.
face to roar.

Press a - long to the Big Cor - ral.

Chuck Wagon
Howard Cook, American, 1901–1980
Lithograph, 1937
MMA

(Please turn the page.)

Actually, few cowboys would ever think of criticizing "cookie"; after all, their sustenance depended on him. They also respected just how hard his job was. He got up "'bout half past four" and prepared a breakfast of strong cowboy coffee (with eggshells in it, to settle the grounds), sourdough biscuits, beefsteak or bacon, and syrup and dried fruit. After the men had eaten—"greased up their gills"—and while they were grazing the stock and then stringing them out in a mile-long trail column, the cook washed up and packed up his portable kitchen, which folded out from a wooden chuck box at the back of the chuck wagon. There was a lot to set out and a lot to put away; for the compact chuck box was uncommonly copious, holding flour, sugar, dried fruit, coffee, pinto beans, plates, cups, cutlery, salt, lard, baking soda, vinegar, chewing tobacco, rolling tobacco, sourdough, matches, molasses, a coffeepot, whiskey, skillets, Dutch ovens, and other implements for outdoor cooking. He hitched his four-mule team to the wagon and rode out ahead of the herd five to seven miles to a spot the trail boss had scouted out, near a stream or other source of water for the cattle. There he prepared the afternoon meal, which the trail hands ate while the cattle drank. After another washup, the cook drove his chuck wagon to the spot designated as the night campsite and prepared the evening meal.

The Lee of the Grub-Wagon
N. C. Wyeth, American, 1882–1945
Oil on canvas, 1904–05
BBHC

THE BIG CORRAL (Continued)

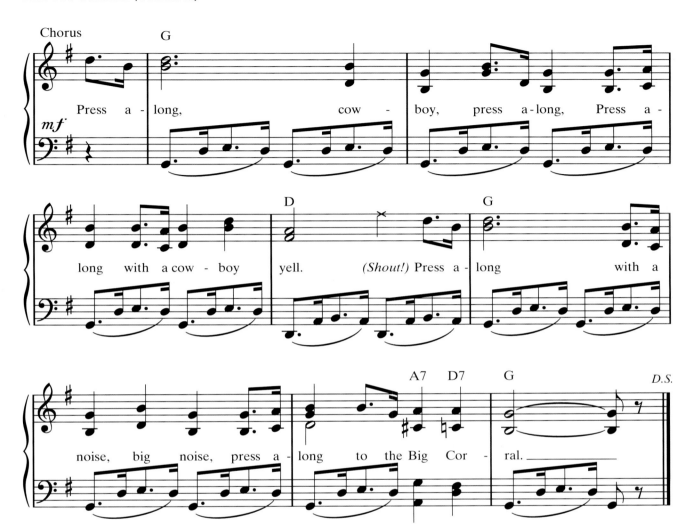

Chorus

Press a-long, cow-boy, press a-long, Press a-long with a cow-boy yell. (Shout!) Press a-long with a noise, big noise, press a-long to the Big Cor-ral.

Additional verses:

3.
The wrangler's out a-combing the hills.
Press along to the Big Corral.
So jump in your britches and grease up your gills.
Press along to the Big Corral.
(Chorus)

4.
The chuck we get ain't fit to eat.
Press along to the Big Corral.
There's rocks in the beans and sand in the meat.
Press along to the Big Corral.
(Chorus)

The painting reproduced here is one of a series of illustrations N. C. Wyeth made to accompany "A Day with the Round-Up," an article published in *Scribner's Magazine* in March 1906. Father of the popular realist artist Andrew Wyeth and grandfather of the painter Jamie Wyeth, Newell Convers Wyeth learned the illustrator's art in the Wilmington, Delaware, studio of Howard Pyle. His western work was done early in his career; *The Saturday Evening Post* published his first illustration, a bucking bronco, in 1903, and *Scribner's* and *Outing* magazines sent him on western assignments over the next three years. Although N. C. Wyeth is probably best known for the wonderful illustrations that appear in Scribner's "Juvenile Classics" series—some twenty-five books—he turned increasingly to fine art late in his career, completing murals for the Missouri State Capitol and the National Episcopal Cathedral in Washington, D.C..

Pot
American, 18th or 19th century
Iron MMA

63

THE STRAWBERRY ROAN

What is a cowboy without a horse? For one thing, he's out of a job. Each working season on the ranch and on the trail, every cowboy required a saddle string of about ten mounts. There was never any shortage of horses in the West, but relatively few were specially bred on ranches. Generally, the ranchers let the animals breed on the range and run wild, rounding them up as needed. Although not even ranch-bred horses are born ready to ride, at least they have plenty of time to get used to the presence of human beings. Range horses, called broncs or broncos, are wholly unused to people, and training—or breaking—them can be a time-consuming and danger-ous process. A bronc has a natu-ral tendency to jettison, forcefully, anyone who climbs on its back.

In the days of the great trail drives, every ranch had a few cowboys called broncobusters, who specialized in breaking animals for use. The only way to do this was to ride the beast—and successfully resist getting thrown.

Bronco Buster
Charles M. Russell, American, 1864–1926
Watercolor on paper, 1915
BBHC

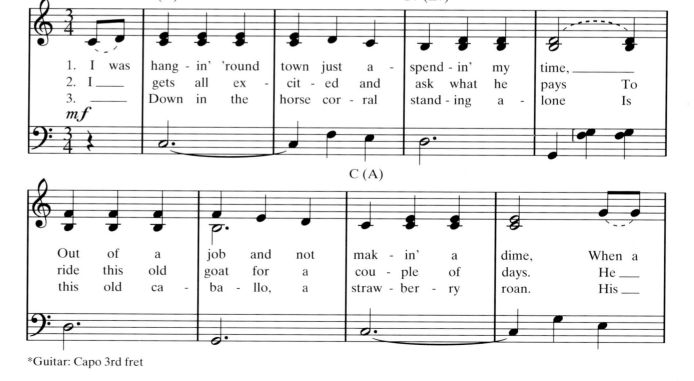

Moderately, with spirit

1. I was hang - in' 'round town just a - spend - in' my time,_____
2. I_____ gets all ex - cit - ed and ask what he pays To
3. _____ Down in the horse cor - ral stand - ing a - lone Is

Out of a job and not mak - in' a dime, When a
ride this old goat for a cou - ple of days. He_____
this old ca - ba - llo, a straw - ber - ry roan. His_____

*Guitar: Capo 3rd fret

64

fel - ler steps up_____ and says, "I sup - pose man, That
of - fers a ten spot; I says, "I'm your man, For the
legs is all spav - ined, he has pi - geon toes, Two

you're a bronc rid - er by the looks of your clothes."
bronc nev - er lived_____ that_____ I could - n't fan. No, the
lit - tle pig eyes_____ and a big Ro - man nose,

"You got me right and a good one," I claim, "Do you
bronc nev - er lived nor he nev - er drew breath That_____
Lit - tle pin ears_____ that touched at the tips, And a

hap - pen to have an - y bad ones to tame?" He
I could - n't ride till he starved half to death." He
big for - ty four_____ run on his left hip. He's

(*Please turn the page.*)

Incorrigible broncs, called out-laws, defeated all efforts at being ridden. A really mean bronc was called a sunfisher, because of a tendency to leap up and twist, as if trying to shine some sun on its belly—hardly a comfortable situa-tion for the would-be rider.

Sally James Farnham, whose sculpture of a sunfisher appears on the following page, was one of the few women artists who special-ized in western subjects. She was not a westerner, however; her home-town, Ogdensburg, New York, was also the birthplace of that most famous and successful of western artists, Frederic Remington, who befriended, advised, and praised her. Remarkably, except for the advice of Remington and two or three other sculptors, Farn-ham was entirely untrained and unschooled as an artist.

Saddling a Wild Horse
Laton Alton Huffman, American, 1854–1931
Hand-colored photogravure, 1905
MMA

Sally Farnham took up sculpting when she was hospitalized after the birth of a child. Bedridden and bored, she began modeling in wax. Shortly thereafter, she opened a studio and became immediately successful.

The Sun Fisher is a small cast bronze, like those her friend Remington became famous for, but Farnham also created monumental works, such as the equestrian statue of Simón Bolívar, the Venezuelan revolutionary, that stands at the south end of New York City's Central Park. Sally Farnham beat out twenty traditionally trained sculptors for that commission.

The Sun Fisher
Sally James Farnham, American, 1876–1943
Bronze, 1920
BBHC

66

THE STRAWBERRY ROAN *(Continued)*

says, "I've got one and a bad one to buck," And at
says, "Get your sad - dle; I'll __ give you a chance." So we
ewe - necked and old, with a long low - er jaw; I could

throw - in' good rid - ers he's had lots of luck."
got in the buck - board and eye he was a rode to the ranch.
see with one reg - 'lar out - law.

Chorus

Well, it's oh, that straw - ber - ry roan!

Oh, that straw - ber - ry roan! _____

They
We
He's

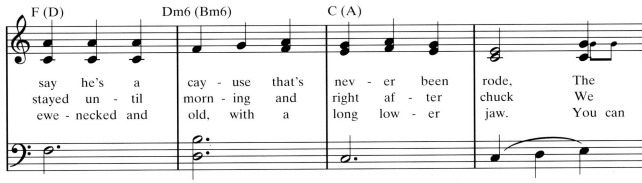

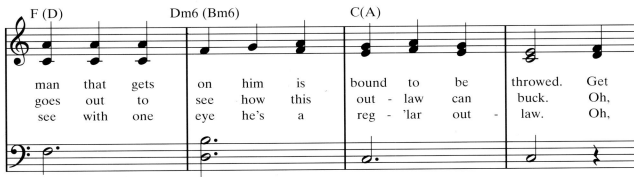

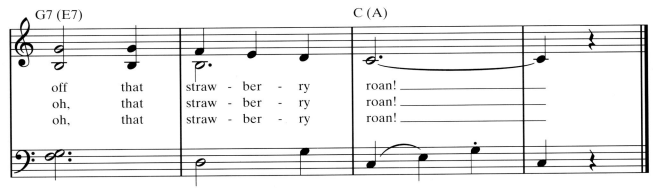

Additional verses:

4. I buckle on my spurs,
   I'm sure feelin' fine,
   I picks up my hat,
   an' curls up my twine.
   I piles my rope on him,
   and well I know then,
   That afore I get rode,
   I've sure earned my ten.
   I gets the blinds on him,
   it sure is a fight,
   Next comes my old saddle,
   an' I screws her on tight.
   Then I steps onto him
   and raises the blinds,
   I'm right in his middle
   to see him unwind.

Chorus
Well, it's oh,
   that strawberry roan!
Oh, that strawberry roan!
He lowered his neck,
   and I think he unwound,
He seemed to quit living
   down there on the ground.
Oh, that strawberry roan!

5. He went up towards the east
   and came down towards the west;
   To stay in the middle
   I'm doin' my best.
   He's the worst bucker
   I've seen on the range:
   He can turn on a nickel
   and give you some change.
   He turns his old belly
   right up to the sun;
   He sure is one sunfishin'
   son of a gun!
   I'll tell you, no foolin',
   this pony can step,
   But I'm still in his
   middle and buildin' a rep.

Chorus
Well, it's oh,
   that strawberry roan!
Oh, that strawberry roan!
He goes up on all fours
   and comes down on his side,
I don't see what keeps him
   from losing his hide.
Oh, that strawberry roan!

6. I loses my stirrup
   and also my hat.
   I starts pulling leather
   I'm blind as a bat;
   With a big forward jump,
   he goes up on high,
   Leaves me sittin' on nothing
   way up in the sky;
   I turns over twice,
   and I comes down to earth,
   I lights in a-cussin'
   the day of his birth.
   I know there is ponies
   I'm unable to ride;
   Some are still living,
   they haven't all died.

Chorus
Well it's oh,
   that strawberry roan!
Oh, that strawberry roan!
I'll bet all my money
   the man ain't alive
That can stay with old strawberry
   when he makes his high dive.
Oh, that strawberry roan!

Cowboy hat
American, ca. 1920
Fur felt, ribbon, and leather
BBHC

67

THE COLORADO TRAIL

All of the great cattle trails were long, and all produced their lonely moments, but the Colorado Trail, which branched off the far more famous and well-traveled Western Trail, was lonelier than most. It did not end at a rowdy cattle town, for it was not a trail to market or railhead but to the rich northern ranges, where young Texas cattle were sometimes taken for fattening long before being driven to market. This song, written on the Colorado Trail, is a lyrical gem that proves cowboys can be poets, and anybody who has ever missed a loved one cannot fail to appreciate the sentiment made more poignant by the economy with which it is expressed.

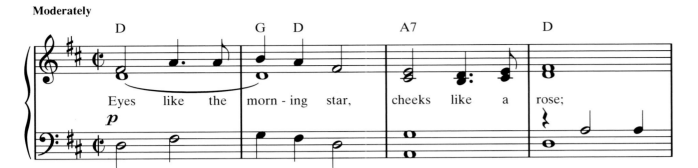

Eyes like the morn-ing star, cheeks like a rose;

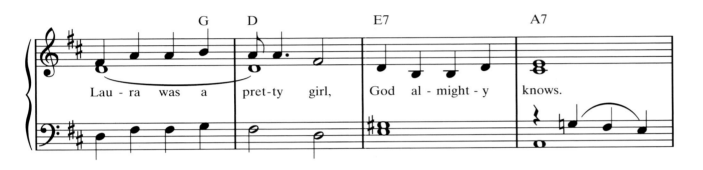

Lau-ra was a pret-ty girl, God al-might-y knows.

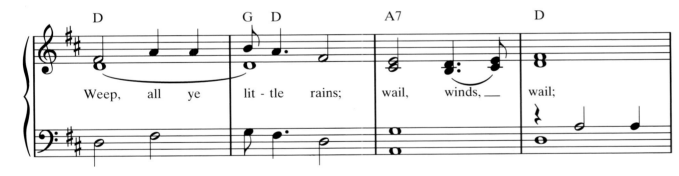

Weep, all ye lit-tle rains; wail, winds, — wail;

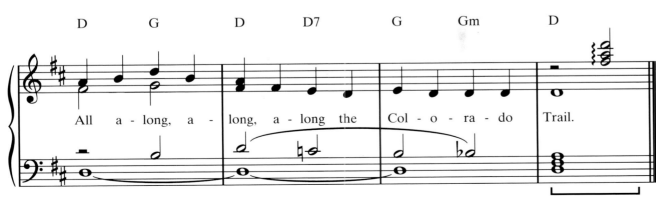

All a-long, a-long, a-long the Col-o-ra-do Trail.

Frederic Remington, best known for his rough-and-tumble paintings of cowboys and cavalrymen in violent action, was also capable of capturing the reflective moments that solitude, prairie, and moonlight engender. The frontier West offered many dangers, but a song like "The Colorado Trail" and a painting like *The Night Rider* suggest yet another challenge, for the vast, open land often forced a man to be alone for long periods of time with his thoughts and his feelings.

The Night Rider
Frederic Remington, American, 1861–1909
Oil on board, ca. 1908   BBHC

Girl with Roses
Probably by Paul Wyttenbach, American, active 1900–1920
Color lithograph, published by Cosmopolitan Lithograph Co., 1912   MMA

A day on the trail ended with the evening roundup, as shown in this hand-colored photogravure, when the grazing herd and the saddle band were gathered and bedded down for the night. Even after their long walk, cattle were often restless at night, and it was the night guard's job to circle round the herd in order to contain them and prevent individuals from drifting off. With luck, the cattle would get up about midnight, stretch, walk around a bit, and then bed down again. Some nights, though, it seemed they would never settle down, and the night guard would have no choice but to ride and ride to bunch the dogies up.

Frank Tenney Johnson, whose painting appears on the opposite page, made moonlit western scenes something of a specialty. He ran away from boarding school to learn painting from F. W. Heinie, a Milwaukee artist. Later, Johnson studied with Richard Lorenz, a Texas Ranger turned artist, and began to do illustration work. Eventually, he moved to New York, where he enrolled in the Art Students League. By the turn of the century, Johnson was concentrating almost exclusively on western scenes.

Evening at the Round-Up Camp, Montana
Laton Alton Huffman, American, 1854–1931
Hand-colored photogravure, 1906
MMA

NIGHT-HERDING SONG

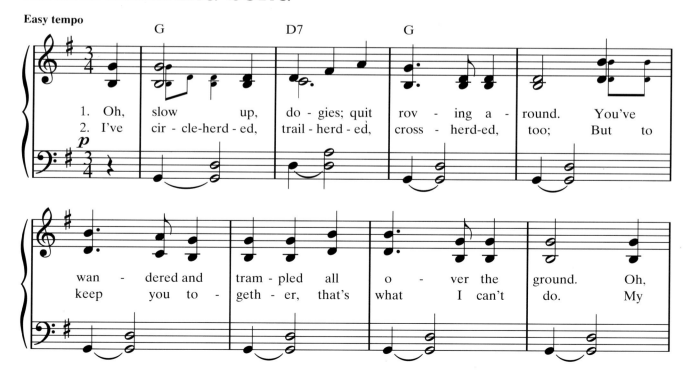

1. Oh, slow up, do-gies; quit rov-ing a-round. You've wan-dered and tram-pled all o-ver the ground. Oh,
2. I've cir-cle-herd-ed, trail-herd-ed, cross-herd-ed, too; But to keep you to-geth-er, that's what I can't do. My

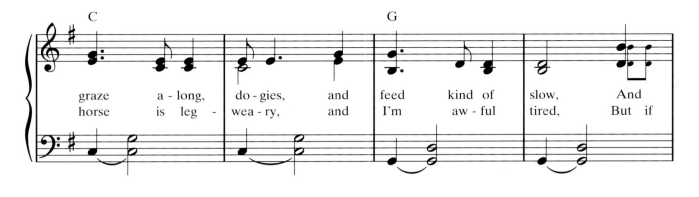

graze a-long, do-gies, and feed kind of slow, And
horse is leg-wea-ry, and I'm aw-ful tired, But if

Additional verses:

3. Oh, say, little dogies,
   when you goin' to lay down
   And quit this forever
   sifting around?
   My limbs are weary,
   my seat is sore;
   Oh, lay down, dogies,
   like you've laid down before.
   Lay down, little dogies, lay down.

4. Oh, lay still, dogies,
   since you have laid down.
   Stretch away out on
   the big open ground.
   Snore loud, little dogies,
   and drown the wild sound;
   They'll all go away
   when the day rolls round.
   Lay still, little dogies, lay still.
   Hi-yoo, he-yoo, woo-oo.

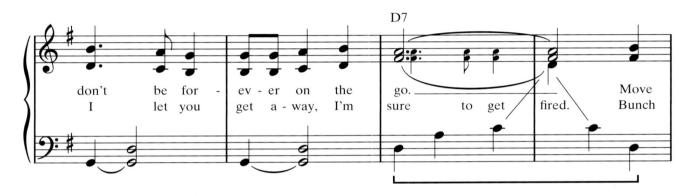

don't be for - ev - er on the go. _____ Move
I let you get a - way, I'm sure to get fired. Bunch

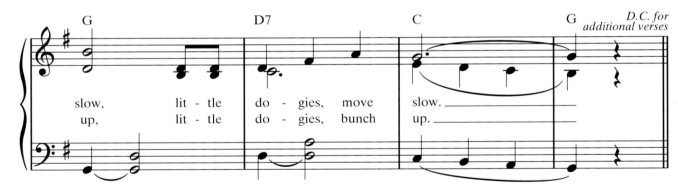

D.C. for additional verses

slow, lit - tle do - gies, move slow. _____
up, lit - tle do - gies, bunch up. _____

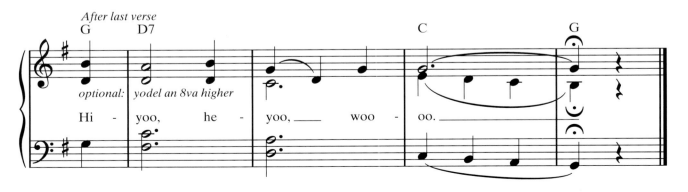

After last verse

optional: yodel an 8va higher

Hi - yoo, he - yoo, _____ woo - oo.

Down the Moonlit Trail
Frank Tenney Johnson, American, 1874–1939
Oil on Masonite, 1938
BBHC

COWBOY LULLABY

Nighttime on the seemingly endless prairies and the vast desert country could be unsettling, both for men and for cattle. It took Emil Bisttram, the Hungarian-born painter of this haunting night scene, some time to get accustomed to the American West. When he first visited Taos, New Mexico—a mecca for many artists of the period—he found himself unable to paint because he was overwhelmed by the "grandeur of the scenery and the limitless space." Soon, however, he became one of the region's most active and successful artists, skillfully blending elements of realism and spiritual fantasy in his most memorable works.

Cowboys trailing cattle to market or fresh pasturage had need of soothing lullabies to calm the herd and thereby avert stampede, lest their charges plunge down an arroyo bank to die. Those cowboys assigned night guard duty had the delicate job of keeping the herd bedded down. The second-shift men, who worked from 11 P.M. to 2 A.M., had the hardest watch, since cattle generally rise, stretch, and walk about at some point during this time.

Easy, loping tempo

1. Des-ert sil-ver blue be-neath the pale star-light, ___
2. Noth-in' out there on the plains that you folks need, ___

Coy-ote yap-pin' la-zy on the hill, ___
Noth-in' there that seems to take your eye. ___

Sleep-y winks of light a-long the far sky-line, ___
Still you got to watch them or they'll all stam-pede, ___

Time for mill-in' cat-tle to be still. ___
Plung-in' down some 'rro-yo bank to die. ___

*Guitar: Capo 3rd fret

(*Please turn to page 74.*)

Rider in the Midnight Sky
Emil Bisttram, American, 1895–1976
Oil on canvas, 1928
MMA

Distant thunder or the howl of a coyote could touch off a stampede, and that meant hours of hard riding to round up strays and coax the herd into a "mill," forcing the cattle to run around in a contracting circle until, exhausted, they bedded down again. Sometimes the cowboys ended up riding in circles all night and, without sleep, had to hit the trail again come morning.

Landscape with Cows
Arthur B. Davies, American, 1862–1928
Watercolor, white and blue crayon, and pencil on blue paper, ca. 1925 MMA

COWBOY LULLABY *(Continued)*

So now the light-ning's far a-way; The coy-ote's noth-in' skeer-y, just sing-in' to her dear - ie. Yah - ho, a - mol-la hol-i-day, So set - tle down, ye cat - tle, till the morn - ing.

BLOOD ON THE SADDLE

O f the working cowboy's requisite ten mounts, only two were fully trained as cutting horses, used for working closely with cattle, for roping, and for cutting steers out of the herd during roundups. The rest of the saddle string was made up of "green-broke" horses, usually four- and five-year-old geldings, fresh off the range, which had been ridden three times by the outfit's broncobuster. Neither a bronc nor a green-broke horse was easy to ride, and some were downright incorrigible, or "wicked," throwing every cowboy who mounted. The lucky would-be riders dusted themselves off and limped away with a few bruises. This song tells us what happened to an unlucky one.

The Wicked Pony
Frederic Remington, American, 1861–1909
Bronze, 1898
BBHC

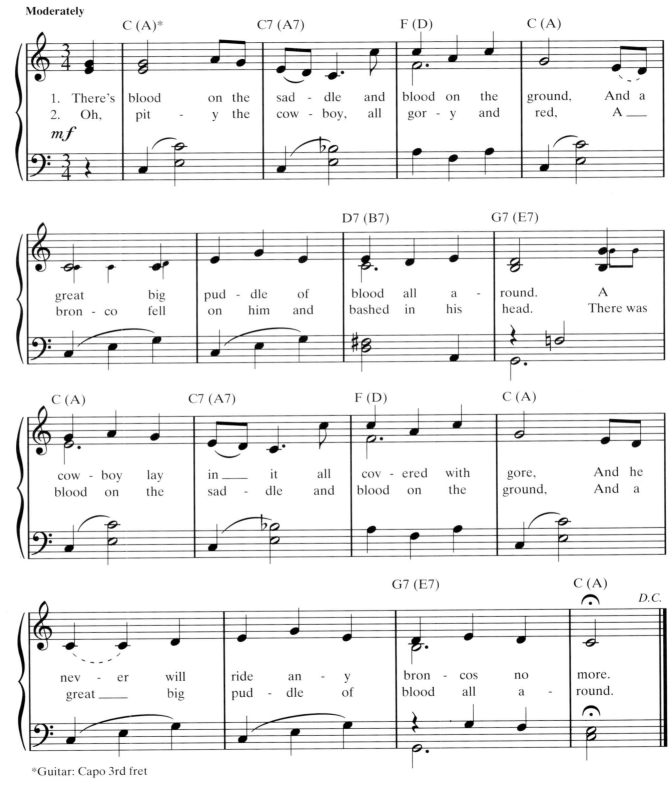

Moderately

1. There's blood on the sad – dle and blood on the ground, And a
2. Oh, pit – y the cow – boy, all gor – y and red, A ___

great big pud – dle of blood all a – round. A
bron – co fell on him and bashed in his head. There was

cow – boy lay in ___ it all cov – ered with gore, And he
blood on the sad – dle and blood on the ground,

nev – er will ride an – y bron – cos no more.
great ___ big pud – dle of blood all a – round.

*Guitar: Capo 3rd fret

75

HOME ON THE RANGE

This is certainly the most famous of all western songs. It has even been dubbed the cowboy national anthem. And who can resist its message of open spaces, freedom, good weather, and good cheer? Interestingly, it is not really a cowboy song at all, and it became popular not in the nineteenth century, but in the twentieth. The song seems to have originated in a poem written in 1873 by a Dr. Brewster Higley, who lived near Smith Center, Kansas. Higley had written, "I would not exchange my home here to range"; by the time western song collector John Lomax recorded the hitherto obscure tune in 1908, the line had been altered to "home on the range."

By 1925, "Home on the Range" was being published in sheet-music form. In 1933, it was the most popular song played on radio. On the night of his election to his first term as president, Franklin Delano Roosevelt declared it his favorite song. Admiral Richard E. Byrd, the great explorer of the Antarctic, said that he played it every day at the South Pole—until his record player froze; then he sang it.

1. Oh, give me a home where the buf-fa-lo roam, Where the deer and the an-te-lope play,_____ Where sel-dom is heard a dis-cour-ag-ing word, And the skies are not cloud-y all day._____

2. How of-ten at night when the heav-ens are bright With the light from the glit-ter-ing stars,_____ Have I stood here a-mazed and asked as I gazed If their glo-ry ex-ceeds that of ours._____

Steers at Play
Lawrence H. Lebduska, American, 1894–1966
Oil on canvas, 1937 MMA

(Please turn the page.)

Expressing in its simplest, most straightforward form the lure of a Golden West, "Home on the Range" might well have been sung by the cowboy, on those days when the freedom of the trail and the limitless sky were exhilarating. It is little wonder that this song enjoyed its first great popularity during the depths of the Great Depression, when gold had turned to lead, when few people felt free, when skies were cloudy all day, and seldom was heard an encouraging word.

George Catlin, whose painting appears on the opposite page, and Albert Bierstadt, whose work appears below, were very different artists. Catlin, for the most part self-taught, approached the West with a sense of mission, to record what he feared would be lost. Bierstadt, who was highly trained, deliberately transformed his landscapes with a deeply emotional romanticism. Despite the artistic gulf that separated them, Catlin and Bierstadt did share a passion to portray, preserve, and communicate the nobility, grandeur, and beauty of the American West.

Buffalo Head
Albert Bierstadt, American, 1830–1902
Oil on paper, mounted on board, ca. 1879
BBHC

HOME ON THE RANGE *(Continued)*

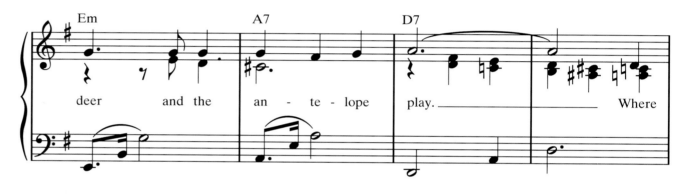

Additional verses:

3. Where the air is so pure, the zephyrs so free,
   The breezes so balmy and light,
   That I would not exchange my home on the range
   For all of the cities so bright.
   (Chorus)

4. Oh, I love those wild flow'rs in this dear land of ours,
   The curlew I love to hear scream.
   And I love the white rocks and the antelope flocks
   That graze on the mountaintops green.
   (Chorus)

Buffaloes (Bulls and Cows) Grazing in the Prairie
George Catlin, American, 1796–1872
Oil on cardboard on bristol board, ca. 1855–70
BBHC

79

CHOPO

We all love tales that celebrate the special bond between men and animals, and the West has produced many songs and stories about the cowboy and his faithful horse. It is true that, riding down "mountains so slipp'ry and steep," a man had need of a surefooted mount—in the odd but charming words of the song, "a safety conveyance." And it is especially true that a good cutting horse was highly prized: one that could work close to cattle at roundup time, when animals had to be cut out of the herd for shipment along the trail to market or distant pasturage. With one end of the cowboy's rope wound hard and fast around the saddle horn and the other looped round the horns of a madly flailing 800-pound steer, a good cutting horse had to be nimble and strong in order to avoid entanglement that would "jerk it down" at great peril to steer, horse, and rider.

Yet, despite this sweet song, cowboys rarely allowed themselves much sentiment about their mounts. Very few cowboys could afford to own a horse; they rode whatever mounts their employer, the rancher, supplied. Five to ten horses were provided for each rider on the typical trail drive.

But, maybe, just maybe, in this equine crowd, a cowboy now and then found a horse to remember and, like the *chico* Chopo, one worth celebrating in song.

1. Through — rock-y ar-ro-yos so dark and so deep, Down the
2. Wheth-er sin-gle or dou-ble or the lead of a team, O-ver

mf

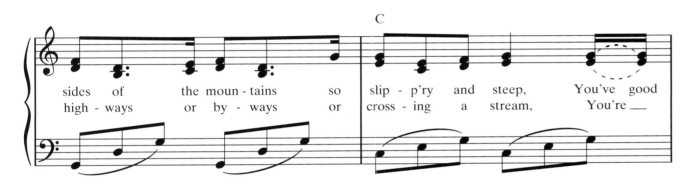

sides of the moun-tains so slip-p'ry and steep, You've good
high-ways or by-ways or cross-ing a stream, You're —

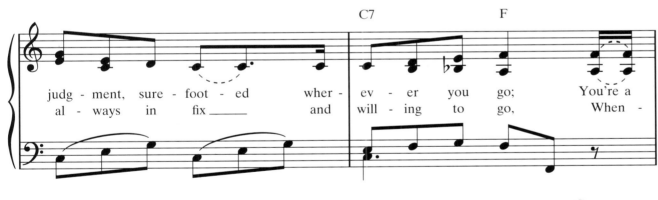

judg-ment, sure-foot-ed wher-ev-er you go; You're a
al-ways in fix — and will-ing to go, When —

safe-ty con-vey-ance, my lit-tle Chop-o.
ev-er you're called on, my *chi-co* Chop-o.

D.C.

Additional verses:

3.
You're a good roping horse;
 you were never jerked down.
When tied to a steer,
 you will circle him round.
Let him once cross the string,
 and over he'll go.
You *sabe* the business,
 my cow horse Chopo.

4.
One day on the Llano,
 a hailstorm began.
The herds were stampeded;
 the horses all ran.
The lightning, it glittered,
 a cyclone did blow,
But you faced the sweet music,
 my little Chopo.

Roping a Cow
Emanuel Wyttenbach, American, 1857–1894
Lithograph, advertisement for H. Royer,
San Francisco   MMA

Rounding Up
N. C. Wyeth, American, 1882–1945
Oil on canvas, 1904–05
BBHC

DOWN IN THE VALLEY

Born in Pittsburgh in 1874 and raised in Cincinnati, Ernest Leonard Blumenschein visited the Taos Valley literally by accident. In 1898, he and a friend, fellow artist Bert Phillips, were traveling from Denver to Mexico when their wagon broke down in the rugged mountain country of New Mexico. The nearest village where they could expect to find a blacksmith to repair their broken wheel was an Indian town called Taos, which Phillips and Blumenschein first glimpsed from a high peak. Blumenschein later recalled that he had been "stirred...deeply" by the sight of the village in the valley and "inspired...to a profound degree...notwithstanding the painful handicap of the broken wheel I was carrying."

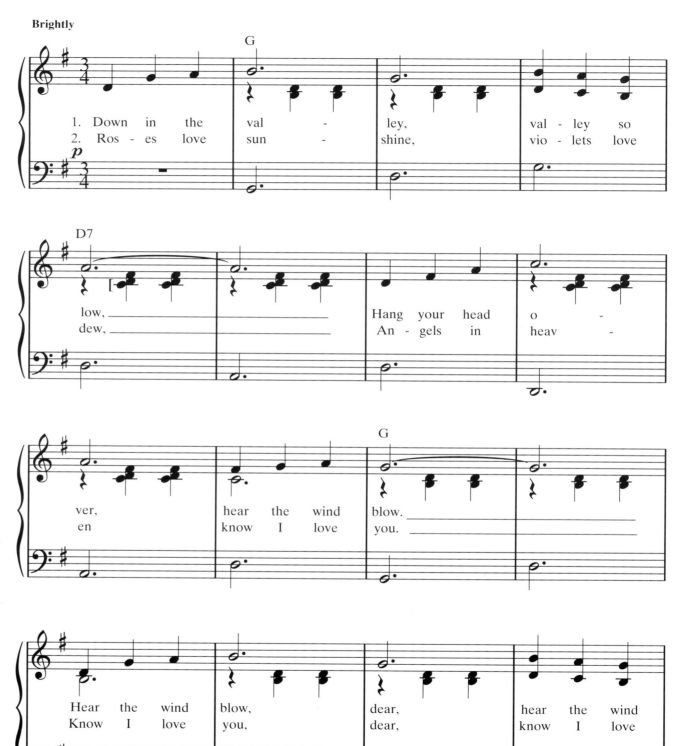

Roses and Violets
Detail of a calling card
American
Color lithograph, late 19th century   MMA

The sender thinks always of thee

Seventeen years after this experience, Blumenschein and Phillips established the Taos Society of Artists, a union of some of the Southwest's most highly regarded painters, including, besides themselves, Joseph Henry Sharp, Eanger Irving Couse, O. E. Berninghaus, W. H. Dunton, and others. These colleagues regarded Blumenschein as the most accomplished artist of their group.

Most certainly, the valley of our song is not the one Blumenschein saw. But it was similarly inspirational, conjuring up peaceful, slightly melancholy thoughts of love. One of the many songs settlers carried with them from the East, "Down in the Valley" furnished welcome images of a familiar landscape to the homesick traveler making the long, long trek across the almost featureless prairie.

8va lower

Taos Valley
Ernest Blumenschein, American, 1874–1960
Oil on canvas, 1933   MMA

THE ZEBRA DUN

Like "Blood on the Saddle" and "The Strawberry Roan," this song celebrates the outlaw—the unbreakable bronc no man can ride. But "The Zebra Dun" has a twist that, like much cowboy humor, is based on poking fun at oneself. A stranger happens on the camp of some range riders. Observing the courteous usages for which the West is justly famed, the cowboys generously offer him breakfast, even though he has the look of a town-bred greenhorn. The stranger starts to talk to his hosts, revealing a breadth of experience far beyond that of most undereducated cowboys; he has even been to Europe. Then this rank tenderfoot asks to borrow a horse, and the boys figure they'll have some fun. They rope an outlaw zebra dun— a buckskin-colored horse with a dark stripe down its back and horizontal zebra stripes on its legs. The stranger saddles up, and the joke, we soon discover, is on the cowboys, who take the stranger's astonishing performance with characteristic good nature.

Bucking
N. C. Wyeth, American, 1882–1945
Oil on canvas, 1904–05
BBHC

Moderately, with humor

1. We were camped up-on the plains __ at the head of the Cim-ar-ron __ When a-
2. We __ asked if he'd had break-fast, but he had — n't had a sniff. __ We __
3. Such an ed-u-cat-ed fel-ler, his thoughts __ just came in herds; He as-

long came a stran-ger __ and he stopped to ar-gue some. __ He
o-pened up the chuck box __ and told him to help him -self. __ He
ton-ished all them punch-ers __ with his jaw-break-ing words. __ He

looked so ver-y fool-ish, we be-gan to look a-round; __ We
took a cup of cof-fee, some bis-cuits and some beans, __ And
just kept on a-talk-ing till he made the boys __ sick, __ And

thought he was a green-horn just es-caped from town. __
then be-gan to talk a-bout for-eign kings and queens. __
they be-gan to fig-ure up some way to play a trick. __

Additional verses:

4. He said he'd lost his job
    up close to Santa Fe,
  And he was going across the plains
    to strike the 7-D.
  He didn't say what the matter was,
    some trouble with the boss,
  But wanted to know if he could borrow
    a fat, fresh saddle horse.

5. This tickled all the boys,
    they laughed down in their sleeves.
  We told him he could have one
    as fresh and fat as you please.
  So Shorty grabbed a lariat
    and roped old Zebra Dun,
  Turned him over to the stranger,
    and waited for the fun.

6. The stranger hit the saddle,
    and old Dunny quit the earth.
  He traveled straight up in the air
    for all that he was worth.
  A-pitching and a-squealing
    and a-having wall-eyed fits,
  His hind feet perpendicular
    and his front ones in the bits.

7. We could see the tops of the mountains
    under Dunny's every jump.
  But the stranger, he was growed there
    just like a camel's hump.
  The stranger sat upon him
    and curled his black moustache,
  Just like a summer boarder
    a-waiting for his hash.

8. The boss who was a-standin' there,
    a-watching of the show
  Went right up to the stranger
    and told him he needn't go.
  "If you can throw a lasso
    like you rode old Zebra Dun,
  You're the man that I've been looking
    for since the year of One."

9. Oh, he could throw the lasso,
    and he didn't do it slow.
  He could catch the forefeet nine out of
    ten for any kind of dough.
  There's one thing and a sure thing
    I've learned since I was born:
  Every educated feller
    ain't a plumb greenhorn.

COTTON-EYED JOE

Bright square dance tempo

1. Tune __ up your fid - dle, Ros - in up your bow, Play a lit - tle tune called
2. If it had-'na been for Cot - ton-Eyed __ Joe, I'd - a been a - mar - ried
3. Come __ for to see you, Come __ for to sing, I come for to get you

Movies and television have taught us that the American cowboy's musical instrument of choice was the guitar. Actually, the banjo was more popular, and if any one instrument can be called the instrument of the frontier, it was the fiddle, which was even more prevalent than the banjo. "It was a poor cow outfit that did not have in its equipment at least one fiddle or banjo, and a man who could play the same," declared one old trail driver. The fact was that the fiddle and the banjo were simply more portable than the guitar, and they were the instruments of the South, the birthplace of many a cowboy.

The westerner used the fiddle at dances, more as a rhythm maker than as a melodic instrument. Whereas a classical violinist holds his instrument high, using his shoulder and the side of his chin, barely supporting the violin's neck with his left hand, the western fiddler wedges the instrument between chin and chest, firmly grasping the neck. This limits the agility of the left hand, but it provides the support needed to saw a strong beat.

The Fiddler
Bill Borron playing the fiddle
Charles Belden, American, 1887–1966
Gelatin silver print
BBHC

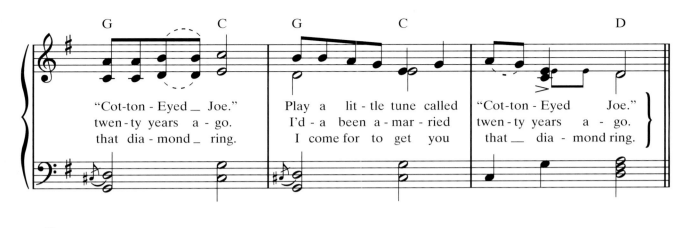

"Cot-ton - Eyed _ Joe."
twen - ty years a - go.
that dia - mond _ ring.

Play a lit - tle tune called
I'd - a been a - mar - ried
I come for to get you

"Cot-ton - Eyed Joe."
twen - ty years a - go.
that _ dia - mond ring.

The lyrics of "Cotton-Eyed Joe" instruct the fiddler to rosin up his bow. Rosin gives a sharp edge to a fiddle's tone, which is just the effect most cowboy musicians wanted. However, rosin was not so easy to come by in the frontier West. Consequently, cowboy fiddlers never cleaned their instruments, but allowed the rosin dust to accumulate above the bridge and beneath the strings. That way, when a fiddler needed to "rosin up," he just dragged the bow across the accumulated powder.

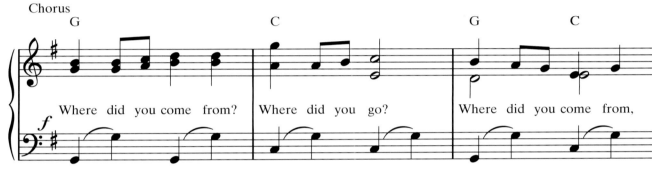

Chorus

Where did you come from?

Where did you go?

Where did you come from,

Cot - ton-Eyed Joe?

Where did you come from,

Cot - ton-Eyed Joe?

Last time

rall.

8va
lower

Folk violin
American, ca. 1900
Maple and poplar   MMA

BUCKING BRONCO

Cowboying is about as manly a profession as there is, and no species of cowboy is more of a man than the broncobuster, who specializes in breaking wild and semiwild horses. But as the bronc rider would tame the horse, so the fair maiden would tame the cowboy — and on that theme has turned many a western tale of romance.

W.H.D. Koerner was called upon to illustrate numerous such stories that appeared in popular magazines, most notably *The Saturday Evening Post*. Born in Lun, Germany, he was brought to Clinton, Iowa, at age two in 1880. He headed for Chicago at sixteen and secured a job as staff artist for the *Chicago Tribune* at the starvation wage of $5 per week. Nevertheless, he managed to attend classes at the Art Institute and the J. Francis Smith Art Academy. Koerner next served briefly as art editor for a magazine in Battle Creek, Michigan, before he came to New York and enrolled in the Art Students League, which he attended from 1905 to 1907. His next stop was Wilmington, Delaware, home of Howard Pyle, the foremost illustrator of his time. Koerner studied with Pyle until 1911.

Morning Ma'am
W.H.D. Koerner, American, 1878–1938
Oil on canvas, 1925   BBHC

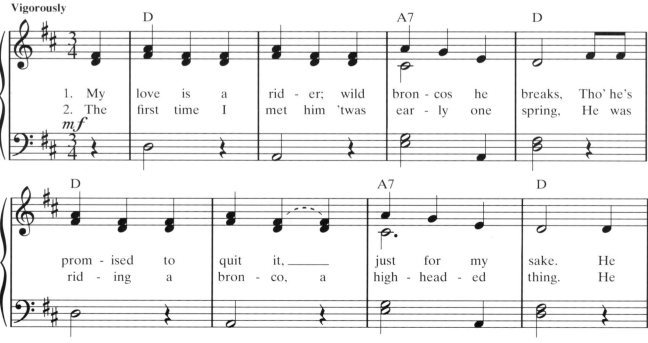

Vigorously

1. My love is a rid - er; wild bron - cos he breaks, Tho' he's
2. The first time I met him 'twas ear - ly one spring, He was

prom - ised to quit it, _____ just for my sake. He
rid - ing a bron - co, a high - head - ed thing. He

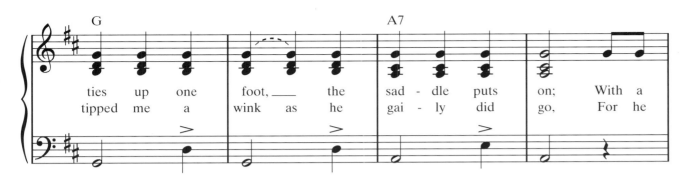

ties up one foot, ___ the sad - dle puts on; With a
tipped me a wink as he gai - ly did go, For he

swing and a jump, he is mount - ed and gone.
wished me to look at his buck - ing bron - co.

By the 1920s, Koerner had ascended to the top ranks of illustrators. Specializing in western subjects, he spent several summers at the Phil Spear Ranch near the Crow Indian reservation in Montana, but his full-time studio and home were back east, in Interlaken, New Jersey.

Additional verses:

3. The next time I saw him 'twas late in the fall,
   Swinging the girls at Tomlinson's ball.
   He laughed and he talked, as we danced to and fro,
   Promised never to ride on another bronco.

4. He made me some presents, among them a ring.
   The return that I made him was a far better thing.
   'Twas a young maiden's heart; I'd have you all know
   He'd won it by riding his bucking bronco.

5. Now all you young maidens, where'er you reside,
   Beware of the cowboy who swings the rawhide.
   He'll court you, and pet you, and leave you, and go
   In the spring up the trail on his bucking bronco.

Breezy Riding
W.H.D. Koerner, American, 1878–1938
Oil on canvas, 1926
BBHC

I RIDE AN OLD PAINT

Even without any lyrics, the easy, loping cadence of this classic song would be enough to conjure up the image of a cowboy meandering down a dusty trail. But the song does have words, and they savor of the West as deliciously as the tune and the rhythm do.

Like many cowboys, our singer rides a pinto, whose name comes from an old Spanish word meaning "spotted" or "painted." Anglo cowboys often called pintos paints. He leads another horse, probably saddled with his pack and all his worldly possessions. Some versions of this song say "old dam" rather than "old Dan," which suggests that the pack horse is the old paint's mother.

Chaps
American, ca. 1900
White angora
BBHC

90

1. I ride an old Paint, I lead an old Dan. I'm off to Mon-tan' for to throw the hoo-li-han. They feed in the cou-lees, they water in the draw; Their tails are all mat-ted, their backs are all raw.

2. Old Bill Jones had two daugh-ters and a song; One went to Den-ver, and the oth-er went wrong. His wife, she died in a pool-room fight, And he sings this song from morn-ing till night:

3. Oh, when I die, take my sad-dle from the wall, Put it on my po-ny and lead him from the stall. Tie my bones to his back, turn our fac-es to the west, And we'll ride the prai-ries we love the best.

(Please turn to page 92.)

Cowboys from the Bar Triangle
Charles M. Russell, American, 1864–1926
Watercolor on paper, 1904
BBHC

The cowboy in this song is bound for Montana, though it's not one hundred percent clear what he intends to do there. For throwing a hoolihan can mean two things. The ropers in Russell's *Cowboys from the Bar Triangle*, which appears on the preceding page, are each about to throw a hoolihan—a quick rope toss to bring a steer down at roundup. So, perhaps, our singer is headed for a Montana roundup in preparation for a trail drive to market. But hoolihan is also a synonym for a rodeo sport called bulldogging— throwing a steer by seizing its horns and twisting its neck until it falls. Maybe, then, he's going to compete in a Montana rodeo. His horses feed in coulees—dry gulches—and drink in the draw—a gully. And the cowboy gently cautions the steers—those little dogies—to give his horses plenty of room, for the fiery (another term for paint) and the snuffy (a buff- or snuff-colored horse) are high-strung and ready for action.

The concluding verses say a lot about cowboy life, too. The second verse is to be sung tongue in cheek, but it does make the point that a cowboy's world could be rude and crude. And verse three, grim though it may be, nevertheless tells us what we expect to hear from a true rider of the range.

I RIDE AN OLD PAINT *(Continued)*

Saddle
American, California-Oregon style, ca. 1895
Leather
BBHC

92

THE RAILROAD CORRAL

Rollicking and spirited

1. We're up in the morn - ing at break - ing of day; The
2. Come take up your cinch - es and shake out of your reins, The Come

chuck wag - on's bus - y, the flap - jacks in play. The
wake your old bron - co and break for the plains. Come

L.H.
herd is a - stir o - ver hill - side and vale, With the
roust out your steers from the long chap - ar - ral, For the

*Guitar: Capo 3rd fret

(*Please turn the page.*)

At the end of the great cattle trails were the cattle towns. Points of transfer from trail to rail, places like Abilene, Dodge City, and Ellsworth, Kansas, were where beef brokers made major purchases on the basis of a handshake and where a cowboy could get a shave, female companionship, a drink, and a game of cards to gamble away his wages in a single night, so that he'd have nothing to show for three or four months on the trail other than his saddle sores.

The cattle, straight from the long drive, were herded into corrals adjacent to the railroad tracks, loaded into cattle cars, and shipped to the great stockyards of the Midwest and East. The cowboys, likewise hot off the trail, were not subjected to similar confinement. As Frederic Remington's *Coming Through the Rye* illustrates, they were, in effect, turned loose on the town and generally went wild. Merchants, innkeepers, saloon owners, and the like grew rich on the trade, and much of it was good, clean fun. But the cattle towns also paid a heavy price in crime, violence, and affronts to public decency. Remarkably, through its first three cattle seasons, Abilene lacked law-enforcement officials of any kind. Concerned citizens passed ordinances forbidding firearms within the city limits and posted signs to that effect. Cowboys thought they made good practice targets.

Coming Through the Rye
Frederic Remington, American, 1861–1909
Bronze; 1902, this cast 1907
BBHC

93

Frank Mechau's painting portrays corralled mustangs rather than cattle, but it does show the great pens and their proximity to the railroad. Mustangs, semiwild horses, were sometimes rounded up for breaking as saddle mounts; more often, however, they were corralled for shipment to slaughter houses.

THE RAILROAD CORRAL *(Continued)*

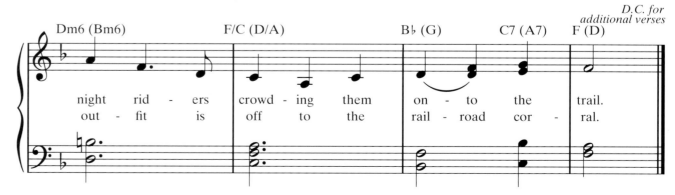

D.C. for additional verses

Dm6 (Bm6)   F/C (D/A)   B♭ (G)   C7 (A7)   F (D)

night rid - ers   crowd - ing them   on - to the   trail.
out - fit is   off to the   rail - road cor - ral.

Additional verses:

3. The sun circles upward,
    the steers as they plod
  Are pounding to powder
    the hot prairie sod.
  And it seems, as the dust
    makes you dizzy and sick,
  That we'll never reach noon
    and the cool shady creek.

4. But tie up your kerchief
    and ply up your nag,
  Come dry up your grumbles
    and try not to lag.
  Come drive out your steers
    from the long chaparral,
  For we're far on the road
    to the railroad corral.

5. The afternoon shadows
    are starting to lean,
  When the chuck wagon sticks
    in a marshy ravine.
  The herd scatters farther
    than vision can look.
  You can bet all the punchers
    will help out the cook.

6. Come shake out your rawhide
    and shake it up fair,
  Come break your old bronco
    and take in your share.
  Come roust out your steers
    from the long chaparral,
  For it's all in the drive
    to the railroad corral.

7. But the longest of days
    must reach evening at last,
  The hills are all climbed
    and the creeks are all passed.
  The tired herd droops
    in the yellowing light;
  Let 'em loaf if they will,
    for the railroad's in sight.

8. So flap up your holster
    and snap up your belt,
  And strap up your saddle
    whose lap you have felt.
  Goodbye to the steers
    from the long chaparral,
  There's a town that's a trump
    by the railroad corral.

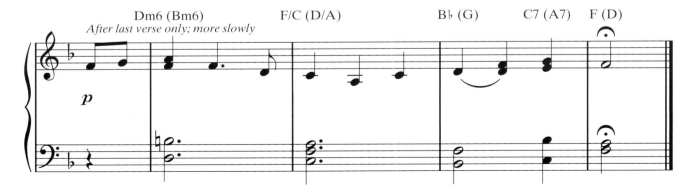

THE COWBOY'S LAMENT

Gunfights were distressingly frequent in western towns. In 1860, for example, the Tucson, Arizona, "Boot Hill" had only two graves that sheltered the remains of men who had died of natural causes. Yet the murder rate in tough western towns like Tucson falls far short of what twentieth-century urban mayhem has produced. In part, this is due to the notorious unreliablity of the early western handgun. Often, it simply misfired or failed to fire, and when it did fire, its unrifled, relatively abbreviated bore could be counted on to launch the bullet on an unpredictable course. Gunfighters who really wanted to kill one another reached for a shotgun or a Winchester rather than a six-gun. William Gollings's action-filled painting notwithstanding, shootouts from the saddle were rare.

Slowly

F (D)* C7 (A7) F (D) C7 (A7)

1. As I _____ walked out in the streets of La - re - do, As
2. "I see by your out - fit that you are a cow - boy." These
3. "Oh, beat the drum slow - ly and play the fife low - ly; —

p

F (D) Bb (G) F (D) C7 (A7)

I _____ walked out in La - re - do one day, I
words he did say as I bold - ly stepped by. "Come
Play the Dead March as you car - ry me a - long. Take me

F (D) C7 (A7) F (D) C7 (A7)

spied a young cow - boy wrapped up in white lin - en, Wrapped
sit down be - side me and hear my sad sto - ry; I'm
to the green val - ley and lay the sod o'er me, For

F (D) Bb (G) F (D) C7 (A7) F (D) *D.C.*

up in white lin - en and cold as the clay.
shot in the breast and I know I must die."
I'm a young cow - boy and I know I've done wrong."

*Guitar: Capo 3rd fret

Additional verses:

4. "It was once in the saddle
   I used to go dashing;
   It was once in the saddle
   I used to go gay.
   First to the dram house
   and then to the card house,
   Got shot in the breast
   and I'm dying today."

5. "Get six jolly cowboys to carry my coffin;
   Get six pretty maidens
   to bear up my pall.
   Put bunches of roses all over my coffin,
   Put roses to deaden
   the clods as they fall."

6. "Go bring me a cup, a cup of cold water
   To cool my parched lips,"
   the young cowboy said.
   Before I returned, the spirit had left him
   And gone to its Maker—
   the cowboy was dead.

7. We beat the drum slowly
   and played the fife lowly,
   And bitterly wept as we bore him along.
   For we all loved our comrade,
   so brave, young, and handsome,
   We all loved our comrade
   although he'd done wrong.

Snare drum
American, 19th century
Wood, skin, and rope MMA

Fight at the Roundup Saloon
William Gollings, American, 1878–1932
Oil on canvas, 1928 BBHC

97

SAM BASS

Unlike wagon trains, which were slow moving but did provide safety in numbers, the lone stagecoach made a tempting target for robbery. The California artist Edward Borein had mixed his art training with odd jobs for local ranchers, an apprenticeship to a saddler, and a stint as a full-fledged cowboy. In this picture, he was as concerned with portraying the authenic details of the old western stagecoach as he was with dramatically conveying the life-and-death business of the robbers or, as they were commonly called, road agents.

The life of Sam Bass (born July 21, 1851; died July 21, 1878) illustrates just how thin the line was that separated the Old West's law-abiding citizens from its ruthless bandits. Orphaned in early childhood, Bass left his native Mitchell, Indiana, in 1869, drifted, and eventually moved to Denton, Texas, in 1870. There Sheriff W. F. Eagan hired him as a farmhand and teamster. The lawman found him a dependable employee; later, Eagan would take part in the manhunt that ended the bandit's career as well as his life.

Holding Up the Stage
Edward Borein, American, 1872–1945
Watercolor on paper
BBHC

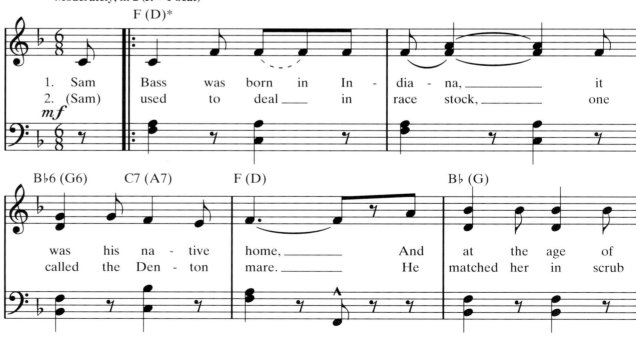

Moderately, in 2 (♩. = 1 beat)

1. Sam Bass was born in In - dia - na, _____ it
2. (Sam) used to deal ____ in race stock, _____ one

was his na - tive home, _____ And at the age of
called the Den - ton mare. _____ He matched her in scrub

*Guitar: Capo 3rd fret

98

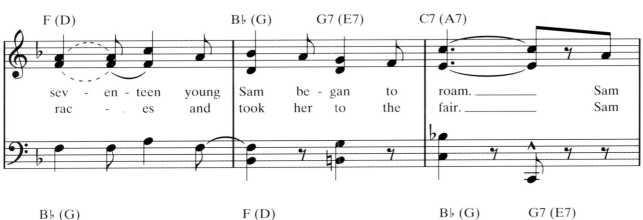

sev - en - teen young | Sam be - gan to | roam. _____ Sam
rac - es and | took her to the | fair. _____ Sam

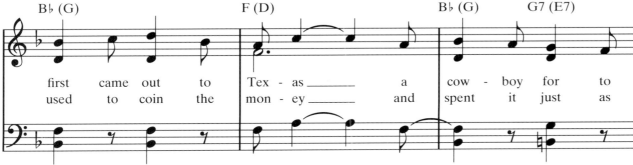

first came out to | Tex - as _____ a | cow - boy for to
used to coin the | mon - ey _____ and | spent it just as

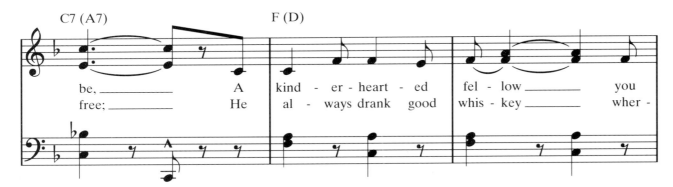

be, _____ A | kind - er - heart - ed | fel - low _____ you
free; _____ He | al - ways drank good | whis - key _____ wher -

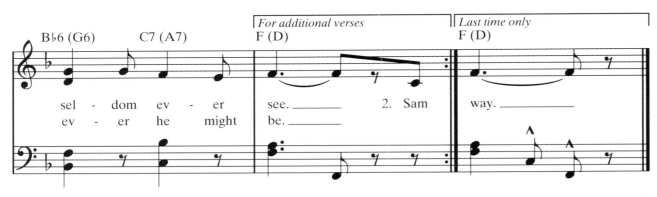

For additional verses   ‖ *Last time only*

sel - dom ev - er | see. _____ 2. Sam | way. _____
ev - er he might | be. _____

(*Please turn the page.*)

After working four years, Bass purchased a racehorse and won a string of ponies from an Indian at Fort Sill, Indian Territory (present-day Oklahoma). When the Indian refused to pay up, Bass seized the herd and rode off to San Antonio. In 1876, Bass teamed up with Joel Collins in cattle, freight, and saloon ventures. The partners amassed sufficient capital to buy a mine. And then they went broke. That is when they crossed the line. After putting together a gang, Bass and Collins spent the ensuing year robbing stagecoaches and railroad trains (a train robbery in Big Spring, Nebraska, September 18, 1877, netted $60,000). In 1878, gang member Jim Murphy betrayed Bass's plan to rob the bank at Round Rock, Texas. Texas Rangers ambushed the bandit in that town on July 19, and he died of gunshot wounds on his birthday, two days later.

Pony Express
The Society of Medalists 45th Issue
James Earle Fraser, American, 1876–1953
Bronze, 1952
MMA

SAM BASS (Continued)

Additional verses:

3. Sam left the Collins' ranch in the merry month of May,
   With a herd of Texas cattle the Black Hills to see.
   Sold out at Custer City and then got on a spree,
   And a tougher set of cowboys you seldom ever see.

4. On their way back to Texas they robbed the U.P. train;
   They then split up in couples and started out again.
   Joel Collins and his partner were overtaken soon,
   With all their hard-earned money they had to meet their doom.

5. Sam made it back to Texas all right side up with care,
   Rode into the town of Denton with all his friends to share.
   Sam's life was short in Texas, three robberies he did do,
   He robbed all the passenger, mail, and express cars too.

6. Sam had four companions, four bold and daring lads,
   Richardson, Jackson, Joel Collins, and Old Dad;
   More bold and daring cowboys the rangers never knew,
   They whipped the Texas Rangers and ran the Boys in Blue.

7. Jim Murphy was arrested and then released on bail,
   He jumped his bond at Tyler and took the train for Terrell
   But Major Jones had posted him and that was all a stall,
   It was a plan to capture Sam before the coming fall.

8. Sam met his fate at Round Rock July the twenty-first,
   They pierced poor Sam with rifle balls and emptied out his purse.
   Sam is now a corpse and six feet under clay,
   And Jackson's on the border still trying to get away.

9. Jim had borrowed Sam's good gold and didn't want to pay,
   The only way he saw it was to give poor Sam away.
   He sold out Sam and Barnes and left their friends to mourn,
   Oh, what a scorchin' Jim will get when Gabriel blows his horn.

10. And so he sold out Sam and Barnes and left their friends to mourn,
    Oh, what a scorchin' Jim will get when Gabriel blows his horn.
    Perhaps he's got to heaven, there's none of us can say,
    But if I'm right in my surmise he's gone the other way.

Buffalo Bill's "Deadwood"
stagecoach
American, 1867
Molded wood with metal supports
and leather interior BBHC

JACK O'DIAMONDS

For untold thousands, the West represented hope and opportunity, but for others, the frontier was at best a place of refuge and, at worst, exile. The singer of "Jack o' Diamonds" is an "old rebel soldier," who, like many southerners, returned from the Civil War only to discover that he had lost property and livelihood. Now too poor to marry his sweetheart, our singer banishes himself to the West— most likely to hire out as a cowboy, a hard, lonely, low-paying job that was the only work available to many a similarly displaced southern lad.

Unhappy men resort to any number of vices, and in the harsh, barely civilized cattle towns of the West, gambling and liquor were prevalent. The combination of cards and whiskey was potentially lethal, as this lithograph by A.C. Radwood illustrates. The seated man, who is being accused of cheating, is a professional gambler—a reasonably respectable trade in the Old West. Of course, such professionals didn't exactly *gamble*. The adept professional knew how to win more often than lose, and the truly successful professional could apply this knowledge without getting into the situation pictured here.

A Call—In Arizona
A. C. Radwood, American, active 1890s
Color lithograph, published by Truth
Company, New York, 1895 MMA

Moderately

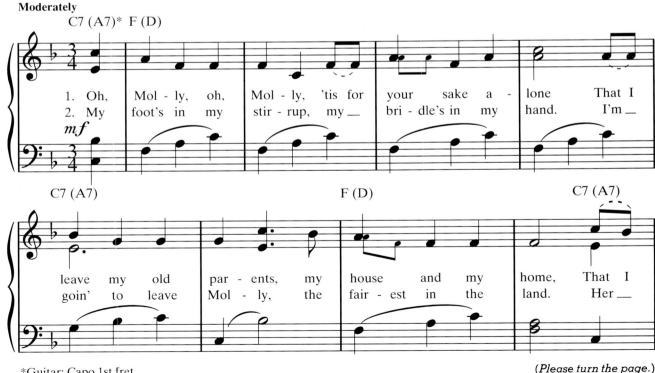

1. Oh, Mol - ly, oh, Mol - ly, 'tis for your sake a - lone That I
2. My foot's in my stir - rup, my bri - dle's in my hand. I'm

leave my old par - ents, my house and my home, That I
goin' to leave Mol - ly, the fair - est in the land. Her

*Guitar: Capo 1st fret

(*Please turn the page.*)

101

JACK O'DIAMONDS *(Continued)*

F (D)

leave my old | par - ents, you | caused me to | roam. I'm an
par - ents don't | like me, they | say I'm too | poor, They ___

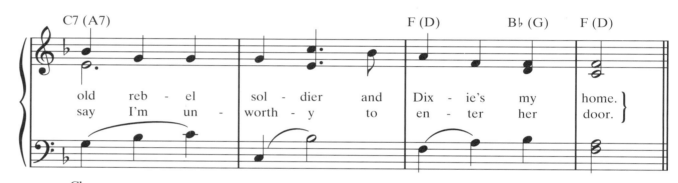

C7 (A7)   F (D)   Bb (G)   F (D)

old reb - el | sol - dier and | Dix - ie's my | home.
say I'm un - | worth - y to | en - ter her | door.

Chorus

C7 (A7)   F (D)

Jack o' | Dia - monds, Jack o' | Dia - monds, I | know you of | old; You've
f

C7 (A7)   F (D)   Bb (G)   F (D)   C7 (A7)

robbed my poor | pock - ets of | sil - ver and | gold. Oh, ___

Old Ramon
Frederic Remington, American, 1861–1909
Color lithograph from *A Bunch of Buckskins:
Eight Drawings in Pastel by Frederic
Remington,* published by R. H. Russell,
New York, 1901 MMA

One of the most famous professional gamblers was Wild Bill Hickok, who became a western legend after serving a brief, violent term as marshal of Abilene, Kansas. Hickok got the job after the town's first marshal, Bear River Tom Smith, a former New York City policeman, was killed while trying to serve an arrest warrant. Wild Bill held the job about half a year before he was fired for being too violent — "only too ready to shoot down, to kill outright," one citizen recalled. That was 1871; five years later, Wild Bill had hung up his guns in favor of a pack of cards. He was playing poker in Saloon No. 10, Deadwood, Dakota Territory, when a drifter named Jack McCall shot him in the back of the head. He died clutching his only winning hand of the afternoon.

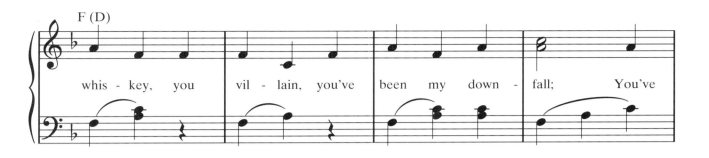

whis - key, you vil - lain, you've been my down - fall; You've

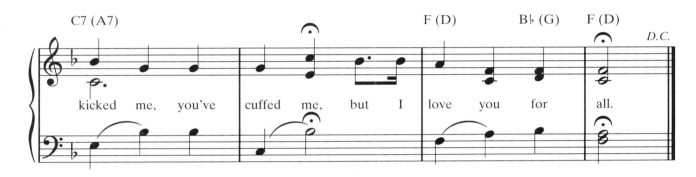

kicked me, you've cuffed me, but I love you for all.

Additional verses:

3. They say I drink whiskey,
   but my money's my own,
   And them that don't like me
   can leave me alone.
   I'll eat when I'm hungry,
   I'll drink when I'm dry,
   And when I get thirsty
   I'll lay down and cry.
   (Chorus)

4. I'll get up in my saddle,
   my quirt in my hand;
   I'll think of you, Molly,
   when in some distant land;
   I'll think of you, Molly,
   you caused me to roam.
   I'm an old rebel soldier
   and Dixie's my home.
   (Chorus)

Rye Whiskey
Advertisement for Sunny Brook whiskey
American
Color lithograph, late 19th century
MMA

Civil War playing cards
Cohen's Patent National Playing Cards
American, ca. 1862
BBHC

THE WELLS AND FARGO LINE

Henry Wells and William G. Fargo, easterners both, formed an express and freighting company in March 1852 to take advantage of the opportunities then burgeoning in California. They established a regular mail, package, and freight route between the East Coast and San Francisco; from San Francisco, they set up branch lines to deliver mail and goods to California's far-flung gold-mining camps.

Much of what the company carried was money and gold dust, and this cargo made Wells Fargo wagons and coaches prime targets for robbery. Of the outlaws mentioned in the song, two can be readily identified. The legendary Black Bart is Charles E. Boles (1830–1917?), who robbed twenty-seven Wells Fargo stages between 1875 and 1882 (using, it was later discovered, an empty shotgun). Jimmy Miner is undoubtedly William ("Old Bill") Miner (1847–1913). Miner ran away from home at age thirteen to become a cowboy, ended up in southern California operating a mail service, and in 1869 tried his hand at robbing a Wells Fargo stagecoach. When his horse stumbled, he was captured, and he served ten years of a fifteen-year sentence in San Quentin. Released for good behavior, Miner teamed up with a highwayman named Bill Leroy and committed many stage and train robberies.

Pass for Gilmer, Salisbury & Co.'s Stage Lines
Emanuel Wyttenbach, American, 1857–1894
Lithograph, 1883   MMA

Brightly

mf

F (D)*

1. Come lis - ten to my sto - ry, I'll not de - tain you
2. Oh, there was Ma - jor Thomp-son, turned up the oth - er

Bb (G)

C7 (A7)

long, A - sing - ing and a - hum - ming this sim - ple sil - ly
day, He said that he would hold them up or the dev - il would be to

F (D)

song. 'Tis of the old ex - con - victs, the
pay. For he could hold a ri - fle and

*Guitar: Capo 3rd fret

104

men who served their time For rob - bing moun - tain
draw a bead so fine Up - on those shot - gun

stag - es on the Wells and Far - go line.
mes - sen - gers of the Wells and Far - go line.

The Virginia City Bodie Stage
Edward Borein, American, 1872–1945
Watercolor on paper   BBHC

Miner spent a year traveling the world, returning to the States by 1880 to rob more stagecoaches. Apprehended in 1881, he served a twenty-year stretch in San Quentin. The middle-aged bandit was released in 1901 but continued to rob trains. In 1905, he was captured and sent to a Canadian penitentiary, from which he escaped (through a thirty-foot tunnel he patiently excavated) in 1907. "Old Bill" robbed a Portland, Oregon, bank in 1909, and a train near White Sulphur, Georgia, in 1911. Captured after this job, he was sentenced to life imprisonment. He broke out three times and was recaptured three times, declaring at last: "I guess I'm getting too old for this sort of thing."

Additional verses:

3. And there was Jimmy Miner
   who thought he was a thief,
   But he did surely prove himself
   to be a dirty sneak;
   And now behind San Quentin's walls
   he's serving out his time,
   For giving tips to old Jim Hughes
   on the Wells and Fargo line.

4. And there was still another
   who well did play his part;
   He's known among the mountains
   as the highwayman, Black Bart.
   He'd ride those mountain jerkies,
   to him it was but pleasure;
   He'd ride the trail both night and day
   for the Wells and Fargo treasure.

5. And now my story's ended,
   I've not detained you long,
   A-singing and a-humming
   this simple silly song.
   And though the nights are long, boys,
   and weary grows the time,
   But when we are out we'll ride again
   the Wells and Fargo line.

BILLY THE KID

Perhaps the most famous of all western gunfighters, Billy the Kid did not, in fact, kill the twenty-one men this song credits him with. In sixteen documented gunfights, Billy killed four men. In the course of robberies, he may have assisted in killing an additional five.

Billy was born Henry McCarty in 1859. When his mother died of tuberculosis in 1874, Billy embarked on a career of petty crime, which soon escalated to murder, when the seventeen-year-old killed a man in a saloon brawl. In 1878, Billy became embroiled in the so-called Lincoln County War, a feud between New Mexico cattlemen, in which he killed the sheriff of Lincoln County.

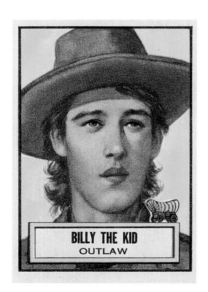

Billy the Kid
Card from the "Roundup" series, published by Topps Chewing Gum
American
MMA

106

A fugitive now, Billy the Kid became a cattle thief and was hunted by Lincoln County's new sheriff, Pat Garrett, to whom he surrendered in December 1880. Four months later, however, Billy evaded the noose by killing his two jailhouse guards and escaping. Garrett ran him to ground at Fort Sumner, New Mexico, on July 14, 1881. Around midnight, Billy entered the adobe house of his supposed friend Pete Maxwell. "That's him," Maxwell said to Garrett, who had entered the house only a few minutes before. The sheriff fired twice at the dimly visible silhouette. The second shot went wild, but the first had found its mark, and Billy the Kid was dead.

Additional verses:

4. 'Twas on the same night
      when poor Billy died,
   He said to his friends,
      "I am not satisfied;
   There are twenty-one men
      I have put bullets through,
   And Sheriff Pat Garrett
      will make twenty-two."

5. Now this is how Billy the Kid
      met his fate:
   The bright moon was shining,
      the hour was late,
   Shot down by Pat Garrett,
      who once was his friend.
   The young outlaw's life
      had come to an end.

6. There's many a man
      with a face fine and fair,
   Who starts out in life
      with a chance to be square.
   But just like poor Billy,
      he wanders astray,
   And loses his life
      in the very same way.

Untitled
V. C. Forsythe, American, 1885–1962
Oil on canvas, 1910 BBHC

JESSE JAMES

After a career of crime that spanned almost two decades, in which he, his brother Frank, and a small gang robbed banks, trains, and even a ticket collector at a county fair (in the process, wounding a little girl in the leg), Jesse James was assassinated on April 3, 1882, by Robert Ford, a new gang member who had joined up with the intention of killing the outlaw and collecting a $5,000 reward. Jesse, who was living in St. Joseph, Missouri, under the name of Thomas Howard, was on a chair adjusting a crooked picture. Ford shot him in the back, and the public cursed him as that "dirty little coward that shot Mr. Howard [and] laid poor Jesse in his grave." When Frank James gave himself up a few months later, the state of Missouri could find no jury that would convict him on any charge. Turned loose, Frank died peacefully in bed more than thirty years later.

The poor, put-upon, and oppressed have always celebrated Robin Hood figures—those who rob from the rich and give to the poor. The fact that there is no evidence that the James boys ever gave anything to anyone didn't much matter to westerners, who perpetually felt themselves victimized by big (eastern-based) government, big (eastern-based) banks, and big (eastern-based) railroads.

Jesse James
Thomas Hart Benton, American, 1889–1975
Lithograph, 1936
MMA

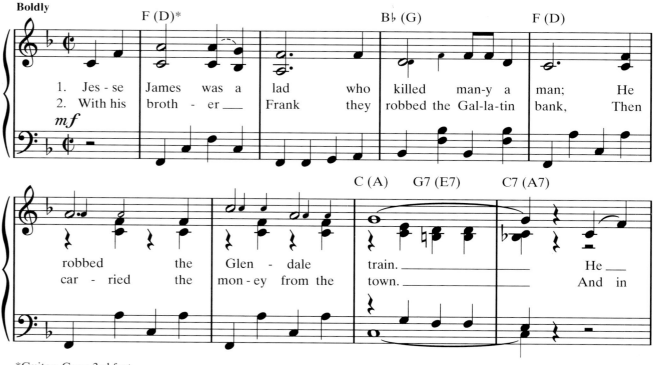

Boldly

F (D)*   B♭ (G)   F (D)

1. Jes - se James was a lad who killed man-y a man; He
2. With his broth - er Frank who they robbed the Gal-la-tin bank, Then

C (A)   G7 (E7)   C7 (A7)

robbed the Glen - dale train. He
car - ried the mon - ey from the town. And in

*Guitar: Capo 3rd fret

stole　　　from the　rich　　and he　gave　　to the　poor, He had　a
this　　ver - y　place _____ they　had a lit - tle　race, _ For they

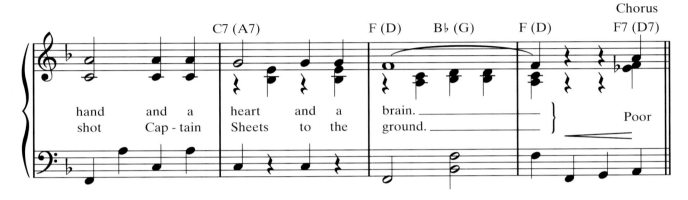

hand　　and a　heart　and a　brain. _____　Poor
shot　Cap - tain　Sheets　to the　ground. _____

Chorus

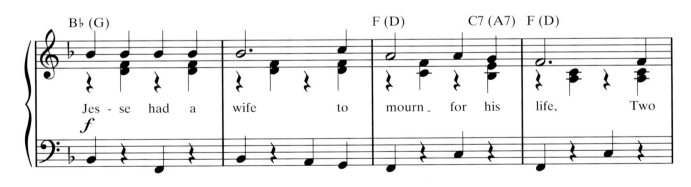

Jes - se had a　wife　　to　mourn _ for his　life, _　Two

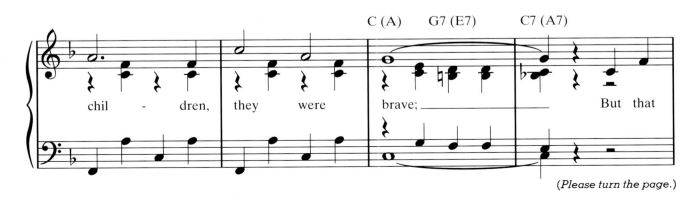

chil - dren,　they　were　brave; _____　But that

(Please turn the page.)

Far from condemning criminals like the Jameses, small ranchers, farmers, homesteaders, and laborers hailed them as Davids battling the Goliaths before whom they themselves were powerless. This ballad is the best-known and most enduring product of the popular mythology that grew up around Jesse and Frank James.

This mythology profoundly affected Thomas Hart Benton, who not only made Jesse James's career the subject of the lithograph reproduced on the opposite page, but, over the objections of some, included Jesse in his titanic mural completed in 1935–36 for the Missouri State Capitol.

Jesse James
Card from the "Roundup" series, published by Topps Chewing Gum
American MMA

JESSE JAMES (Continued)

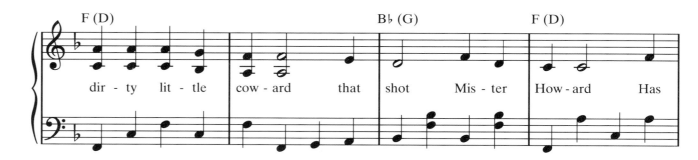

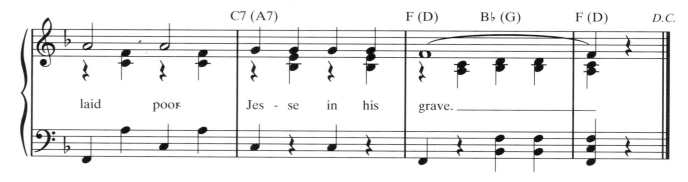

dir - ty lit - tle cow - ard that shot Mis - ter How - ard Has laid poor Jes - se in his grave.

Additional verses:

3.
It was on a Wednesday night, the moon was shining bright.
They robbed the Glendale train.
And the people they did say for many miles away,
It was robbed by Frank and Jesse James.
(Chorus)

4.
They went to a crossing not very far from there,
And here, once again, they did the same.
With the agent on his knees, he delivered up the keys,
To Frank and his brother Jesse James.
(Chorus)

5.
It was Robert Ford, the dirty little coward,
I wonder how he does feel.
For he ate of Jesse's bread, and he slept in Jesse's bed,
Then he laid Jesse James in his grave.
(Chorus)

6.
It was on a Saturday night, poor Jesse was at home,
Talking to his family brave.
Robert Ford watched his eye, and shot him on the sly,
And he laid Jesse James in his grave.
(Chorus)

7.
The people held their breath when they heard of Jesse's death,
And wondered how he ever came to die.
Robert Ford's pistol ball brought him tumbling from the wall.
For he shot poor Jesse on the sly.
(Chorus)

8.
Jesse went to his rest with his hand upon his breast.
The Devil will be down upon his knee.
He was born one day in the county of Clay,
And he came from a solitary race.
(Chorus)

9.
This song was made by Billy Gashade
Just as soon as the news did arrive.
He said there was no man with the law in his hand
That could take Jesse James when alive.
(Chorus)

Jesse James: The Holdup,
Daring Robbery,
Crossfire and *Sneak Attack*
Cards from the "Roundup" series,
published by Topps Chewing Gum
American MMA

110

BUFFALO GALS

"**B**uffalo Gals" is not a uniquely western song; it was known in the Ozarks and the Midwest first, but it traveled west with the cowboys, who made it very popular at square dances and play parties—social occasions for ranchers and cowboys, often sponsored by a local church, usually featuring chaperoned young ladies, and always devoid of intoxicants (discounting what the occasional enterprising cowpuncher might smuggle in).

Bright square dance tempo

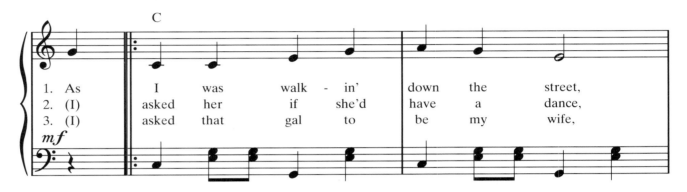

1. As   I   was   walk - in'   down   the   street,
2. (I)   asked   her   if   she'd   have   a   dance,
3. (I)   asked   that   if   gal   to   be   my   wife,

Down   the   street,   down   the   street, A   pret - ty   lit - tle girl   I
Have   a   dance,   care   to   dance. I   thought _ that _ I   might
Be   my   wife,   be   my   dance. I'd   be   so   ver - y   hap - py

A Grand Fandango
Illustration from *The Life and Adventures of Kit Carson* by DeWitt C. Peters, ca. 1858
BBHC

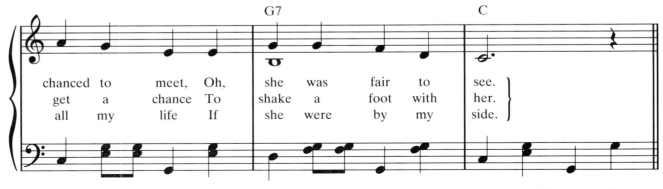

chanced   to   meet, Oh,   she   was   fair   to   see.
get   a   chance To   shake   a   foot   with   her.
all   my   life   If   she   were   by   my   side.

(*Please turn the page.*)

111

If any young woman deserves to be dubbed a Buffalo Gal, it is Phoebe Ann Moses, whose stage name was Annie Oakley. No less a personage than the great Teton Sioux chief Sitting Bull bestowed on her yet another name, *Watanya cicilia*, popularly translated as Little Sure Shot.

Phoebe's father died when she was six; by eight, she had learned to shoot and helped support her destitute family by supplying game to a Cincinnati hotel. In 1875, the hotel owner staged a shooting match between the fifteen-year-old Phoebe and Frank Butler, a vaudeville marksman. Phoebe won and a year later married Butler, with whom she began touring as Annie Oakley.

When Buffalo Bill Cody saw her shoot at the Cotton Exposition in New Orleans in 1884, he hired her for his Wild West Show. For the next seventeen years she shot cigarettes out of Frank Butler's mouth and dimes from between his fingers. Her skill at skeet shooting was no less phenomenal. Two clay pigeons were released, then Oakley would leap over a table, pick up her rifle, and blast apart both targets. In one demonstration with a rifle, she hit 943 of 1,000 glass balls tossed in the air. In another contest, this time with a shotgun, she blasted 4,772 glass balls out of 5,000 during nine hours of continuous shooting.

Miss Annie Oakley,
The Peerless Lady Wing-Shot
Poster, color lithograph, ca. 1890
BBHC

BUFFALO GALS *(Continued)*

Chorus

Buf-fa-lo gals, won't you come out to-night? Come out to-night?

Come out to-night? Buf-fa-lo gals, won't you come out to-night And

Verses 1 and 2
Verse 3

dance by the light of the moon? 2. I moon. Oh,
3. I

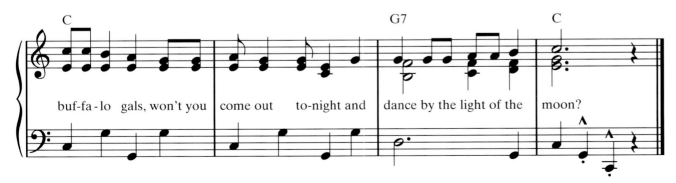

buf-fa-lo gals, won't you come out to-night and dance by the light of the moon?

Annie's career was almost ended by a train wreck in 1901, which left her with severe internal injuries, but after several operations she recovered and not only resumed shooting, but also appeared in stage plays. Although she was born in Ohio and never lived in the West, her marksmanship convinced the American public that she was the typical western girl. Annie died in 1926, at age sixty-six.

Equally famous, but hardly as straitlaced, was Calamity Jane. Born Martha Canary in about 1852, Calamity spent much of her time in and around Deadwood, Dakota Territory, where she may charitably be described as a free spirit, who could out-shoot, out-drink, and out-cuss most any man. Unlike Annie Oakley, she was a bona fide westerner; but, like her, she appeared in Wild West shows. Her reputation was spread far beyond Deadwood by fanciful depictions in popular dime novels, where she was pictured as a lovely buckskin-clad lass devoted to a hero known as Deadwood Dick.

Calamity Jane: Sharpshooting
Card from the "Roundup" series, published by Topps Chewing Gum
American
MMA

113

THE BOLL WEEVIL

Think of the West, and you think big: vast landscapes, bottomless canyons, mountains rising above the clouds, prairies spreading far beyond the horizon, mile-long columns of 800-pound Longhorn steers. But a tiny and very homely insect also played a momentous role in western history. In 1892, the boll weevil—*Anthonomus grandis*—crossed the Rio Grande from Mexico into Texas. The hot, dry climate of much of Texas was ideal for raising cotton, and the state's farmers invested heavily in the crop. When the weevils came, disaster followed. They not only eat cotton, but they lay their eggs in the plant's seed pod—called a boll or square—thereby destroying it: "The first time I saw that weevil/ He was sittin' on the square./ The next time that I saw him/ He had all his fam'ly there."

Potato Bugs
Henry Koerner, American, b. 1915
Pen and ink on paper, 1948
MMA

Moderately, with a lilt (♩♩ played as ♩♪)

1. The boll wee-vil is a lit-tle black bug, Come from Mex-i-co, they say. Came
2. The first time I saw that wee-vil___ He was sit-tin' on the square. The
3. The last time I saw that wee-vil___ He had set-tled down for life; He'd

all the way to Tex-as, Just a-He had
next time that I saw him un-cles, His___
brought his aunts and cou-sins___ and his

look-in' for a place to stay.
all___ his___ fam-'ly there. } Just a-look-in' for a home,_____
cou-sins___ and his wife.

Just a-look-in' for a home,_____ Just a-look-in' for a

114

home, _____ Just a-look-in' for a home. _____

The Thomas Hart Benton painting reproduced here is *Cotton Pickers, Georgia*—but a weevil is a weevil, east or west, and the insect wreaked such havoc not only on Texas cotton but throughout all of the cotton-growing states that one authority has dubbed it the "most costly insect in the history of American agriculture."

Less notorious is the potato bug—actually, like the so-called boll weevil, a beetle—which ruined many western potato crops during the mid-nineteenth century. Native to the Rockies, particularly Colorado, the potato bug was content to feed on various wild tubers until settlers planted the domestic potato in its range. The beetle thrived on this new food and, like the boll weevil, spread from west to east, reaching New York state by 1872.

Cotton Pickers, Georgia
Thomas Hart Benton, American, 1889–1975
Tempera and oil on canvas, 1928–29
MMA

THE WABASH CANNONBALL

It is no accident that the term some Plains Indian groups applied to the railroad locomotive — the Iron Horse — quickly became a cliché. There was something live and animal-like about the colorful mid–nineteenth-century trains. They harnessed two vividly palpable forms of energy — fire and steam — and turned them into equally vivid and visible movement. Like great arms, muscular pistons and drive rods moved the iron wheels. Even the whistle sounded human; indeed, the engineer was said to "play" his whistle, and most railroad men cultivated musical styles so distinctive that, from the distant sound alone, a knowledgeable listener could name engineers he had never even met.

America abounds with affectionate railroad songs like this. The railroad companies were often seen as criminally voracious, snatching up government grants and public lands, but the trains themselves, wondrously forging a union out of states diverse in people and separated by vast distances, were more often celebrated as benevolent, beastlike iron demigods. For the cowboy, though, the ever-expanding railroad heralded the end of his era, for this new and efficient transport gradually took the place of the great cattle drives.

Starting very slowly

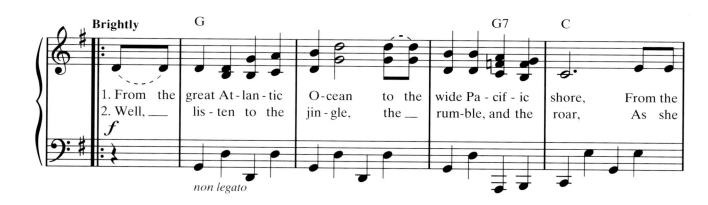

1. From the great At - lan - tic O - cean to the wide Pa - cif - ic shore, From the
2. Well, ___ lis - ten to the jin - gle, the ___ rum - ble, and the roar, As she

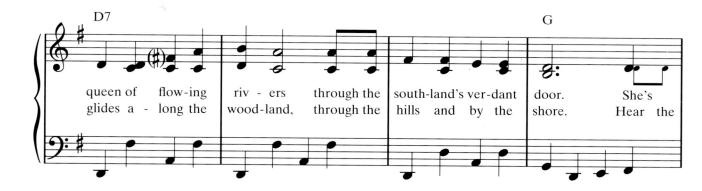

queen of flow - ing riv - ers through the south-land's ver-dant door. She's
glides a - long the wood-land, through the hills and by the shore. Hear the

Currier & Ives, throughout much of the nineteenth century America's most important publisher of popular images, turned out numerous railroad prints to satisfy the public's seemingly insatiable appetite for such lithographs. Frances Flora Bond (Fanny) Palmer, who drew *Across the Continent*, was one of the company's most prolific artists.

might-y tall and hand-some, and __ known quite well by all;
might-y rush of en - gine and the lone - some whis-tle's call;
}
She's the

reg'-lar com-bi - na-tion of the Wa - bash Can - non - ball.

Across the Continent
Frances Flora Bond Palmer, American, ca. 1812–76, for Currier & Ives
Hand-colored lithograph, 1868
MMA

GOODBYE, OLD PAINT

As "I Ride an Old Paint" and this song demonstrate, the paint horse—characterized by a coat showing irregular white areas that appear to have been splashed on like paint—was regarded with considerable affection in the West. This particular song was a favorite of Charley Willis, an ex-slave who became a Texas cowboy about 1871. Willis taught the song to Jess Morris, a hand on the vast XIT ranch, who later formed a popular cowboy orchestra and, in old age, actually recorded "Goodbye, Old Paint" for John Lomax, the nation's most famous collector of western songs. This popular song traditionally was sung at the end of cowboy dances.

African Americans like Charley Willis were not rarities in the ranks of the cowboy; in fact, during the height of the trail-drive era, one in seven cowboys was an African American. Ex-slaves mostly, these men turned to cow-punching as the only work available to them. Despite a great deal of prejudice directed against them, even their most racist white colleagues had grudgingly to acknowledge their skill at working with cattle. Other ethnic groups who turned to the cowboy's trade were Mexicans (who represented about one-seventh of the cowboy population) and Native Americans.

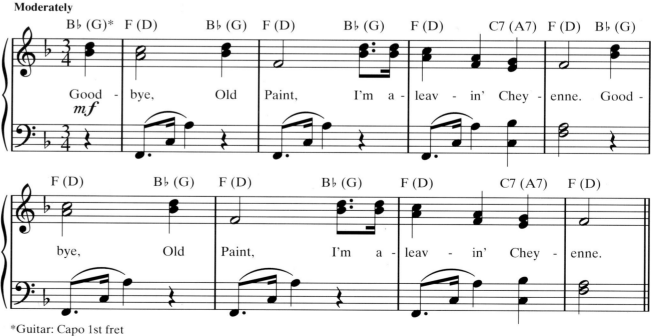

*Guitar: Capo 1st fret

118

F (D)

C7 (A7) F (D)

1. My foot's in the stir - rup, my po - ny won't stan', ___ I'm a-
2. Old Paint's a good po - ny, he pac - es when he can, ___ Good-

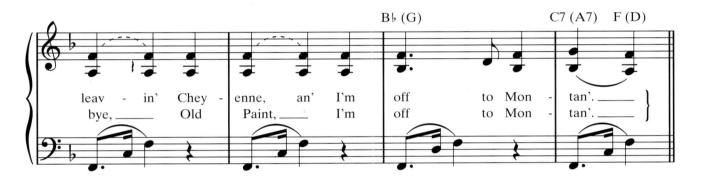

Bb (G)

C7 (A7) F (D)

leav - in' Chey - enne, an' I'm off to Mon - tan'. _____
bye, ___ Old Paint, ___ I'm off to Mon - tan'. _____

Chorus

Bb (G) F (D)   Bb (G) F (D)   Bb (G) F (D)   C7 (A7) F (D)   Bb (G)

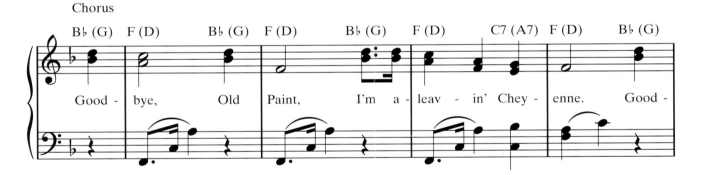

Good - bye, Old Paint, I'm a - leav - in' Chey - enne. Good-

Last time, slower

F (D)   Bb (G) F (D)   Bb (G)   F (D)   C7 (A7) F (D)

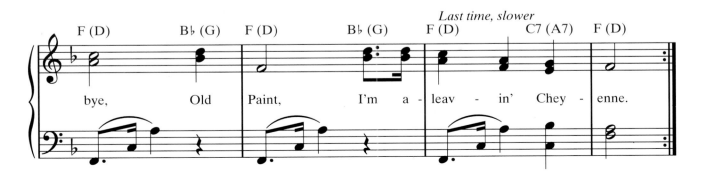

bye, Old Paint, I'm a - leav - in' Chey - enne.

Additional verses:

3. Go hitch up your horses
   and feed 'em some hay,
   An' set yourself by me
   as long as you'll stay.
   (Chorus)

4. My horses ain't hungry,
   they won't eat your hay;
   My wagon is loaded
   and rollin' away.
   (Chorus)

5. My foot's in the stirrup,
   my bridle's in hand,
   Goodbye, Old Paint,
   my horses won't stand.
   (Chorus)

End of the Open Range
Grant Speed, American, b. 1935
Bronze, 1973
BBHC

Horses in the Rain
Robert Noel Blair, American, b. 1912
Watercolor on paper, 1939
MMA

119

THE TEXAS COWBOY

In 1886, Charlie Russell and Jesse Phelps were wintering 5,000 head of cattle for the firm of Kaufman and Stadler. The range-cattle industry—the business of raising beeves on ranges remote from the marketplace and "trailing" the animals to distant railheads for shipment—was at its peak. Ranchers had severely overstocked the range to meet demand. The result was a vast herd of poorly fed, weakened cattle. When the catastrophic winter of 1886–87 hit hard, the cattle began to die: Almost nine out of every ten perished.

Cattleman Kaufman wrote to ask how his firm's cattle were surviving. Russell took a scrap of paper and painted a starved steer in a snowdrift, eyed by hungry wolves. He titled the sketch *Waiting for a Chinook*—a dry wind off the mountains, which would bring a break in the weather. "Send 'em that," he told Phelps.

While Kaufman and Stadler were horrified by its message, they admired the painting, and displayed it in their offices. Russell was asked to paint many copies, and in about 1903 he produced this larger version of the scene. The original was also reproduced commercially. It marked the end of the range-cattle business, but the start of Charlie Russell's tremendously successful career as a western artist.

Moderately

1. Oh, I'm a Tex-as cow-boy so far a-way from home. If
2. I've worked down in Ne-bras-ka where grass grows ten feet high, And

I get back to Tex-as, I nev-er-more shall roam. Mon-
cat-tle are such rust-lers they sel-dom ev-er die. I've

ta-na is too cold for me, the win-ters are too long. Be-
worked up in the Sand Hills and down up-on the Platte, Where

fore the round-ups do be-gin our mon-ey is all gone.
cow-boys are good fel-lows and cat-tle al-ways fat.

120

WAITING FOR A CHINOOK

C M Russell

The Last of 5000

Waiting for a Chinook
Charles M. Russell, American, 1864–1926
Watercolor on paper, ca. 1903
BBHC

Additional verses:

3. I've traveled lots of country, from Nebraska's hills of sand
   Down through the Indian Nation and up the Rio Grande.
   But the badlands of Montana are the worst I've ever seen,
   The cowboys are all tenderfeet and the dogies are too lean.

4. Now all you Texas cowboys, this warning take from me:
   Don't come up to Montana to spend your money free.
   But stay at home in Texas where there's work the whole year round,
   And you'll never get consumption from sleeping on the ground.

OLD TEXAS

Even before the great blizzard of 1886–87 wiped out eighty to ninety percent of range cattle, effectively bringing to a close the days of the great trail drives from Texas ranges to the railheads of Kansas and Missouri, the forces of civilization were competing with cowboy and cattle for the Great Plains. On May 27, 1862, President Abraham Lincoln signed into law the Homestead Act, authorizing any citizen or immigrant who intended to become a citizen to select any surveyed but unclaimed parcel of public land up to 160 acres, settle it, improve it, and, by living on it five years, gain title to it. Accordingly, houses were built and fences erected; by the 1870s, these fences were made of a new, cheap, and highly effective invention called barbed wire. While cattlemen used barbed wire to fence off—illegally—portions of public range land for their private use, homesteaders employed it to mark off their tracts of land and to protect their crops from the pounding hooves of trail-driven cattle. Either way, the open range was being cut up and closed off. Moreover, the multiplication of rail lines in the later nineteenth century, with more numerous railheads being established closer to ranches throughout the West, was making the long-distance trail drive obsolete. Finally, as beef became more plentiful during the quarter-century following the Civil War, the public taste for it became more refined.

122

Ghosts of the Past
Frederic Remington,
American, 1861–1909
Oil on canvas, ca. 1908
BBHC

The rangy Longhorn, with tough, sinewy meat, was being displaced by cattle breeds that yielded a more tender and flavorful steak.

What was a range-riding cowboy to do as his old familiar century drew to the end of its trail? He could accept ranch work, which still meant tending cattle but not driving them any distance. He could accept farm work, which usually did not suit his restless spirit. He could become a laborer, which suited it even less. Or he could "leave old Texas" and try to find a place, like Mexico, where he could be more than a ghost of the past, where a hard but independent life on the trail was still possible.

123

A Fight in the Street
Frederic Remington,
American, 1861–1909
Illustration from *Century*,
October 1888, from *Frederic
Remington, 1861–1909: Artist
Historian of the Old West*, scrapbooks
compiled by Helen L. Card MMA

CREDITS

Front cover:
Buffalo Bill Historical Center
Gifts of John M. Schiff 1.77, 2.77, 44.83
Back cover:
The Metropolitan Museum of Art
Fletcher Fund, 1925 25.97.5
Endpapers:
The Metropolitan Museum of Art
The Elisha Whittelsey Collection,
The Elisha Whittelsey Fund, 1948 48.120.401
Page 1:
The Metropolitan Museum of Art
Thomas J. Watson Library, Helen L. Card Collection
Title page:
The Metropolitan Museum of Art
George A. Hearn Fund, 1938 38.172
Page 5:
The Metropolitan Museum of Art
Thomas J. Watson Library, Helen L. Card Collection
Page 6:
The Metropolitan Museum of Art
Rogers Fund, 1979 1979.380
Page 7:
Buffalo Bill Historical Center
Gift of The Coe Foundation 10.70
Page 8, left:
The Metropolitan Museum of Art
The Crosby Brown Collection of
Musical Instruments, 1889 89.4.2631
Page 8, right:
The Metropolitan Museum of Art
Gift of George S. Amory, in memory of his wife,
Renée Carhart Amory, 1966 66.738.15

Page 9:
The Metropolitan Museum of Art
Rogers Fund, 1907 07.123
Page 10:
The Metropolitan Museum of Art
Gift of the sons of William Paton, 1909 09.214.1
Page 12:
The Metropolitan Museum of Art
Gift of Miss Maryann Bruno, 1942 42.77.2
Page 13, left:
The Metropolitan Museum of Art
Bequest of Adele S. Colgate, 1962 63.550.204
Page 13, right:
The Metropolitan Museum of Art
Gift of the Society of Medalists, 1953 53.12.2
Page 14:
Buffalo Bill Historical Center
Gertrude Vanderbilt Whitney Trust Fund
Purchase 3.60
Page 15:
The Metropolitan Museum of Art
Amelia B. Lazarus Fund, 1910 10.228.2
Page 16:
Buffalo Bill Historical Center
Gift of Mr. and Mrs. Irving H. "Larry" Larom
NA.111.14
Page 17, left:
The Metropolitan Museum of Art
The Michael C. Rockefeller Memorial Collection,
Bequest of Nelson A. Rockefeller, 1979
1979.206.1039

Page 17, right:
The Metropolitan Museum of Art
Gift of Mr. and Mrs. Walter C. Crawford, 1979
1979.491.1
Page 18:
The Metropolitan Museum of Art
Rogers Fund, 1907 07.79
Page 19, left:
The Metropolitan Museum of Art
Gift of Mrs. Russell Sage, 1909 10.225.599w
Page 19, right:
The Metropolitan Museum of Art
Thomas J. Watson Library, Rogers Fund, 1901
Page 20:
Buffalo Bill Historical Center
Gift of the artist 1.59
Page 22, left:
The Metropolitan Museum of Art
The Elisha Whittelsey Collection,
The Elisha Whittelsey Fund, 1948 48.120.251
Page 22, right:
The Metropolitan Museum of Art
The Elisha Whittelsey Collection,
The Elisha Whittelsey Fund, 1948 48.120.113
Page 23:
The Metropolitan Museum of Art
Gift of Several Gentlemen, 1911 11.192
Page 24:
Buffalo Bill Historical Center 1.69.2239
Page 25:
Buffalo Bill Historical Center
Gertrude Vanderbilt Whitney Trust Fund
Purchase 2.60
Page 26:
The Metropolitan Museum of Art
Gift of Miss Maryann Bruno, 1942 42.77.2
Page 27:
Buffalo Bill Historical Center
Given in Memory of William R. Coe and
Mai Rogers Coe 8.66
Page 28:
The Metropolitan Museum of Art
Gift of Miss Maryann Bruno, 1942 42.77.2
Page 29:
The Metropolitan Museum of Art
Gift of Mrs. William F. Milton, 1923 23.77.1
Page 30:
Buffalo Bill Historical Center 25.77
Page 31:
The Metropolitan Museum of Art
The Jefferson R. Burdick Collection,
Gift of Jefferson R. Burdick
Page 33:
The Metropolitan Museum of Art
Bequest of Mrs. H. O. Havemeyer, 1929
H. O. Havemeyer Collection 29.100.596
Page 34:
Buffalo Bill Historical Center
Charles Belden Collection P.67.428D
Page 35:
The Metropolitan Museum of Art
Museum Accession, 1962 62.715
Page 36:
The Metropolitan Museum of Art
Gift of Mrs. Howell Howard, 1956 56.57
Page 37:
The Metropolitan Museum of Art
Hugo Kastor Fund, 1957 57.76
Page 38:
The Metropolitan Museum of Art
Rogers Fund, 1907 07.80
Page 39:
The Metropolitan Museum of Art
Gift of the Friends of the Artist, by subscription,
1912 12.227

Thirsty Oxen Stampeding for Water
Frederic Remington, American, 1861–1909
Illustration from *Century*, July 1891, from *Frederic Remington, 1861–1909: Artist Historian of the Old West*, scrapbooks
compiled by Helen L. Card
MMA

INDEX OF FIRST LINES

Head of a Bull
Emanuel Wyttenbach, American, 1857–1894
Lithograph   MMA

127

GUITAR CHORD DIAGRAMS

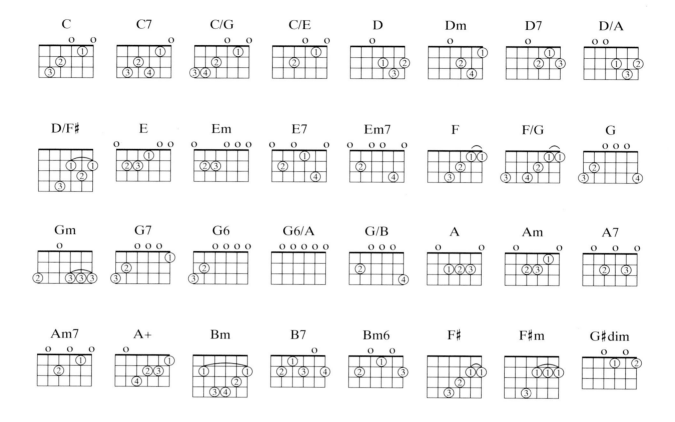

C C7 C/G C/E D Dm D7 D/A

D/F♯ E Em E7 Em7 F F/G G

Gm G7 G6 G6/A G/B A Am A7

Am7 A+ Bm B7 Bm6 F♯ F♯m G♯dim

Coyote and Skull
Frederic Remington, American, 1861–1909
Illustration from *St. Nicholas*,
December 1889, from *Frederic
Remington, 1861–1909:
Artist Historian of the Old West*,
scrapbooks compiled by Helen L. Card
MMA